VICTORY 1940

The Battle of Britain

AS NEVER SEEN BEFORE

JOHN DIBBS & TONY HOLMES

KEY
Books

Published by Key Books
An imprint of Key Publishing Ltd
PO Box 100, Stamford, Lincs, PE19 1XQ
www.keypublishing.com

Editor: Allan Burney. Original production: The Plane Picture Company (planepicture.com) and Narcosis Media. Layout and pre-production: John M. Dibbs and Philip Hempel. Paperback edition: SJmagic DESIGN SERVICES, India. Concept and design © John M. Dibbs and Allan Burney. All colour photography © John M. Dibbs.

ISBN 978 1 913295 08 9

If the British Empire and its
Commonwealth last for a thousand years,
men will still say,
'This was their finest hour'

WINSTON CHURCHILL

Introduction

From the earliest age I knew my future was in history. I can remember being enthralled by the stories of Spitfires and Hurricanes scrambling from RAF Northolt, told to me by my father who grew up right by the Fighter Command airfield's perimeter fence, a witness to the dramatic events unfolding in the summer of 1940.

Whilst inspired by his words, I also recall the frustration at not being able to see for myself what happened that momentous summer. Thus the concept for *Victory 1940* was born, to bring to life the events, actions and human experiences of one of history's most pivotal moments in a bold new way. To make this happen, this book had to be both authentic and an experience.

Famous images that you might know have been meticulously restored to create a window through time. These are complemented by previously unpublished photographs, such as those by Adolf Galland's trusted adjutant who documented the life and losses of Jagdgeshwader 26 based on the Channel Front, some of these images actually carrying Galland's handwritten notes, scribbled on the back during that defining summer.

The fabric of human experience is woven into Tony Holmes' text, with first person accounts taking you to the skies to do battle in Spitfires, Hurricanes and Messerschmitts. At the same time, Simon Smith's art recreates the duelling of Aces all those summers ago. And the final piece in the puzzle being the timeless razor-sharp colour of the beautifully restored aircraft that fly today, airframes that saw combat in 1940 and still serve as a tribute to the Few. We hope you find this mix as intoxicating as the sweet smell of the first coughs of a Merlin engine kicking into life and that you too are carried aloft with those that lived, and tragically died, in the blue summer skies of 1940.

We must not forget.

JOHN M. DIBBS

Contents

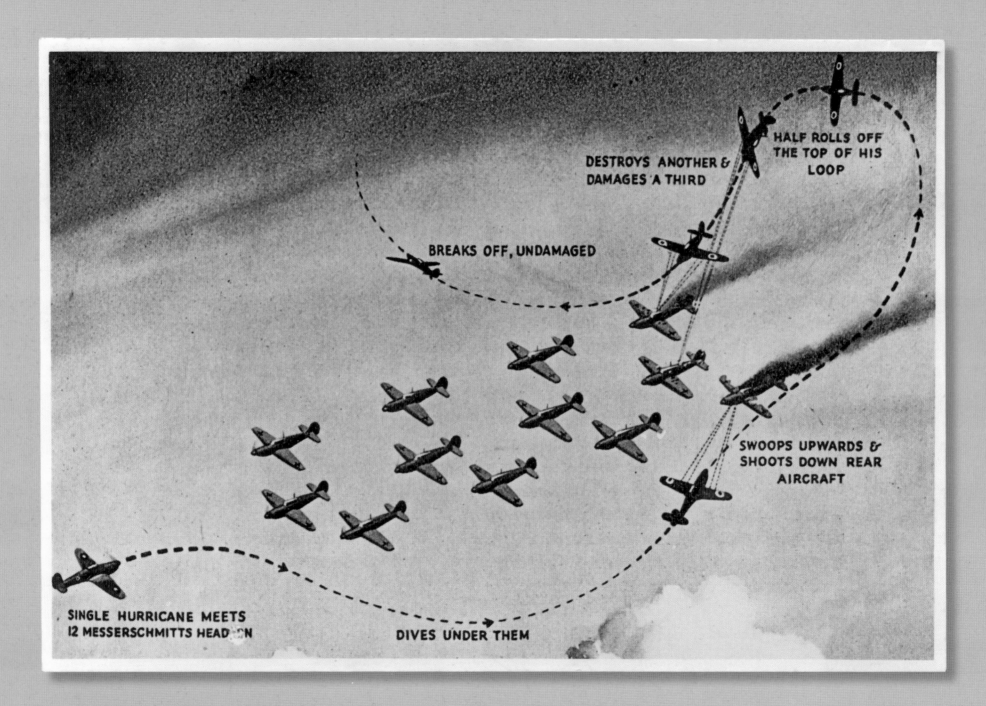

HALF ROLLS OFF THE TOP OF HIS LOOP

DESTROYS ANOTHER & DAMAGES A THIRD

BREAKS OFF, UNDAMAGED

SWOOPS UPWARDS & SHOOTS DOWN REAR AIRCRAFT

SINGLE HURRICANE MEETS 12 MESSERSCHMITTS HEAD ON

DIVES UNDER THEM

FOREWORD

When recently the anniversary of the Battle of Britain became a universal subject of discussion, memories of events many years past drifted through my mind. Particularly that of the afternoon of 4 July 1940, when, aged 19 years of age and a founder member of No 249 Squadron, I was scrambled to intercept a Dornier 17 bomber, some 20 miles off the coast of Yorkshire. I would like to record that, with my two companions, we shot it down, but we didn't; it was far too clever for us and escaped into cloud when, inexperienced as we were, we followed too rigidly the advice given in the 'Fighter Command Instruction Manual' and kept hindering each other.

We did better on the 8th, however, when we shot down a Junkers 88, which we forced down over land, killing the unfortunate pilot and wounding at least one other member of the crew of four. It didn't really help, however, when on the Movietone News a few days later, the Ju 88 was described as being the victim of a Spitfire flying from North Yorkshire, as we happened to be flying Hurricanes from South Yorkshire! Or that a local farmer's wife received most of the credit in the press and later awarded the MBE for attacking the helpless German aircrew with a pitch fork. Such was the aura surrounding the Spitfire, the ignorance (and bravery) of the farmer's wife, and my first experience of how facts could, and would continue to be, distorted in war.

Shortly after this incident, the squadron moved south to Boscombe Down, Wiltshire, which was in No 10 Group. There the controlling was very poor and we suffered our first casualties, my own personal Hurricane being lost and my close friend and Flight Commander, James Nicolson, one of three pilots shot down over Southampton by attacking Me 110s. His Hurricane in flames, wounded and badly burnt, he remained in his cockpit to continue firing his guns and fatally damage the 110 which had overtaken him. After which, although he managed to bale out successfully, he was shot at again by a sergeant in the British Army who, in a panic, mistook him for an invading enemy parachutist. For his gallant contribution in this engagement, Nicolson was decorated in November 1940, with the one and only Victoria Cross awarded to a pilot in Fighter Command during the Second World War.

On 1 September, No 249 Squadron moved up to North Weald in Essex where we were to stay throughout the rest of the Battle and experience some very trying moments. These included enduring two heavy bomber attacks on our airfield; taking part in over 150 massed scrambles and interceptions; and the several occasions when our squadron of 18 Hurricanes was reduced to five serviceable aircraft. We were also greatly saddened by the loss of eight colleagues and friends killed, and 22 wounded, burnt or otherwise incapacitated.

In the 16 weeks between 10 July and 31 October, I flew 141 times against the enemy and lost four Hurricanes, but apart from one parachute jump and some frights, holes and a few bruises, remained comparatively unscathed. More than a few of my surviving colleagues, alas, suffered mental and physical injuries that were to haunt them all their lives.

It was also made painfully evident to all of us at the time, the shortcomings as well as the virtues of our early Spitfires and Hurricanes, the many imperfections in our training methods and tactics, and in particular our poor marksmanship and the inadequacy of our armament of eight machine guns and their meagre 15 seconds-worth of ammunition.

It revealed, too, some of the reasons we did not lose the Battle! These include the organisation of the warning and control system in Fighter Command, the manner in which our squadrons were almost miraculously resupplied daily (we were never short of aircraft), the devotion to duty (and to us, their pilots) of our ground staff, and the spirit of my colleagues and friends, who never once in my hearing, uttered a single word of despair or defeat.

And, the other side of the coin - the Luftwaffe always being obliged to fight over enemy territory, which resulted in their losses, compared with ours, seldom being less than two-to-one. They, too, fought with courage.

It is against this background and the need to implant in the minds of the young, the gallantry and sacrifices of those who fought in the Battle of Britain, that this valuable book, *Victory 1940*, should be read and enjoyed. John Dibbs' collection of meticulously restored wartime imagery as well as his beautiful air-to-air photographs of surviving examples of aircraft that flew throughout that momentous year, serves as a truly fitting tribute to the combatants on both sides.

Tom Neil

249 Sqn

WG CDR TOM NEIL, DFC*, AFC

The ROAD to BATTLE
Prelude, Blitzkrieg, Dunkirk

....

"Delays have
Dangerous ends"

King Henry the Sixth, Act III, Scene II

William Shakespeare

Prelude

The roots of the Battle of Britain, fought during the long hot summer of 1940, go back further than the outbreak of World War 2 in September of the previous year. Germany felt great animosity towards Britain and France in particular because of the punitive and humiliating defeat it had been forced to agree to at Versailles in June 1919 following its capitulation in World War 1. Saddled with a swingeing reparations bill (132 billion gold marks) and the loss of territory including the Saarland and Alsace Lorraine, the average German harboured resentment and a deep desire for revenge. Unsurprisingly, a charismatic politician promising to satiate these desires through the restoration of national glory eventually rose to power.

A veteran of fighting on the Western Front, Adolf Hitler and his National Socialist German Workers' Party, commonly known as the Nazi Party, emerged from the German nationalist, racist and populist Freikorps paramilitary culture, which fought for control of the country against the communist uprisings in post-World War 1 Germany. Party leader from 1921, Hitler led the Nazis into power when it became the largest force in the German Reichstag following a series of elections in 1932. Once he became Chancellor in 1933, Hitler was now the effective head of government. Indeed, he combined the offices of President and Chancellor when he became Führer in August 1934.

By then Germany had already withdrawn from the League of Nations Disarmament Conference in October 1933 and secretly formed a new air force, the Luftwaffe. The first steps towards its formation had been undertaken just months after Hitler came to power. Hermann Göring, a highly decorated World War 1 ace, became National Kommissar for aviation, with former Deutsche Lufthansa director Erhard Milch as his deputy. In April 1933 the Reichsluftfahrtministerium (Reich Air Ministry – RLM) was established, this organisation being put in charge of development and production of aircraft. Göring's control over all aspects of aviation became absolute.

German rearmament and militarisation gathered speed to such an extent that it prompted complaints from neighbouring countries in Europe, which in turn commenced their own rearmament programmes to defend themselves from what they saw as inevitable Nazi aggression in the coming years. These nations had cause to be alarmed, for when the Luftwaffe's existence was announced on 27 March 1935 by Hitler, he boasted that it already had parity with the Royal Air Force – not an entirely true statement, as most of the German aircraft were in fact trainers. Hitler stated that his intention was to match the French Armée de l'Air, which was then the largest air arm in western Europe.

As Germany's armed forces swelled in size, so did the country's appetite for expansion. One of Hitler's driving ambitions had been to re-establish a 'Greater Germany', whose borders were roughly equivalent to those that had existed prior to the Treaty of Versailles. He duly achieved this without bloodshed through a plebiscite in the Saarland in January 1935 and violation of the Locarno Pact, forbidding the militarisation of the Rhineland, in March 1936. Few protested these moves as most European governments viewed these areas as being 'rightly German' in any case. Encouraged by this lack of opposition, Hitler annexed Austria – the country of his birth – in the so-called 'Anschluss' (the Nazi propaganda term for the country's incorporation into Germany) of March 1938. Once again, because the Austrians were a Germanic people, speaking German and supporting the Nazis, there was little international opposition to the move.

Six months later Hitler sent the Wehrmacht into the Sudetenland, the northern, southwest and western areas of Czechoslovakia that were inhabited primarily by German speakers. The word Sudetenland had in fact only existed since the early 20th century, attaining prominence after World War 1 when, after the German-dominated Austro-Hungarian empire had been dismembered, the Sudeten Germans found themselves living in newly created Czechoslovakia. Hitler knew he was taking a gamble in seizing Sudetenland, as many of his advisors believed that he would be opposed by Britain and France.

However, Hitler's bold strategy paid off when, instead of demanding the removal of German forces from Czechoslovakia, the British and French governments 'forced' the Nazis to sign up to the Munich Agreement. This settlement permitted Germany's annexation of portions of Czechoslovakia along the country's border areas that were primarily inhabited by German speakers in exchange for a guarantee of the nation's sovereignty – Hitler agreed not to invade the rest of Czechoslovakia. The settlement was negotiated on 29 September 1938 at a conference held in Munich that was attended by the major powers of Europe, excluding the Soviet Union and, critically, Czechoslovakia. The agreement, signed by Germany, France, the United Kingdom and Italy, robbed Czechoslovakia of most of its border defences and much of its heavy industry.

When British Prime Minister Neville Chamberlain returned to London from the negotiations in Munich, he proudly waved a copy of the Munich Agreement at the assembled crowd and proclaimed 'peace in our time'. Whether he believed this or not was irrelevant, for Britain's armed forces were totally unprepared for war at that point.

In March 1939 the Wehrmacht occupied the rest of Czechoslovakia, its border defences having been compromised by the loss of the Sudetenland the previous year. Despite Germany having no legitimate claim to the sovereign nation, the international community and, specifically, the signatories of the Munich Agreement did nothing. By turning a blind eye to Hitler's latest land grab, Britain and France in particular all but condemned Poland to the same fate.

The final piece in the Führer's reunification puzzle was the German-speaking port of Danzig and the corridor of territory that separated the German exclave of East Prussia from the rest of the Reich. The so-called Polish Corridor was a strip of land that had been long disputed by Poland and Germany and inhabited by a Polish majority. Although the Corridor became a part of Poland after the Treaty of Versailles, many Germans living in the city of Danzig and its environs wanted the area to be reincorporated into Germany. It had been separated from Germany after Versailles and made into a nominally independent Free City of Danzig. Hitler sought to use his demands for reunification as a reason for war, appealing to German nationalism by promising to 'liberate' the German minority still in the Corridor, as well as in Danzig.

The subsequent invasion of Poland during the early morning of 1 September was referred to by Germany as the '1939 Defensive War'. Indeed, Hitler proclaimed that the Poles had attacked Germany and that 'Germans in Poland are persecuted with a bloody terror and are driven from their homes. The series of border violations, which are unbearable to a great power, prove that the Poles no longer are willing to respect the German frontier'. This time, however, after Hitler had ignored an ultimatum given to him by the British government to withdraw his troops by 3 September, much to his astonishment the governments of Britain and France fulfilled their treaty obligations with Poland and declared war on Germany.

The propaganda slogan 'Ein Volk, Ein Reich, Ein Führer!' (One People, One Nation, One Leader!) was used to great effect by the Third Reich.

Produced in 1938, this shocking poster was created by the Spanish Republican government following the Nationalist bombing of Madrid. Franco's Nationalists were supported with munitions and personnel by Hitler in the form of the Condor Legion, where many future Luftwaffe aces honed their combat skills.

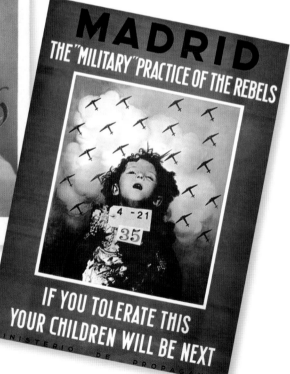

'The British Ambassador in Berlin handed the German Government a final Note stating that, unless we heard from them by 11 o'clock that they were prepared at once to withdraw their troops from Poland, a state of war would exist between us.
I have to tell you now that no such undertaking has been received, and that consequently this country is at war with Germany'

NEVILLE CHAMBERLAIN

The crew of an He 111P pore over maps prior to conducting an exercise during the summer of 1938. Typically, a Heinkel crew consisted of a pilot, navigator, bomb aimer and both ventral and dorsal gunners.

NEIGHBOURLY CONDUCT

Herr Hitler. "Extraordinary how the least little bit of noise seems to upset some parties."

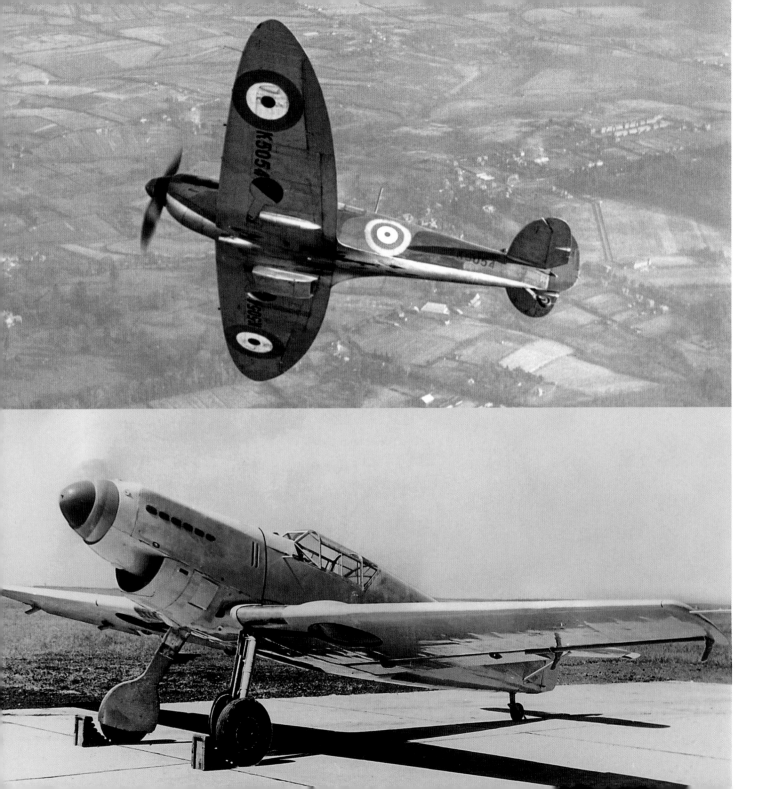

A member of the Hitler Youth receives tuition from a Nationalsozialistisches Fliegerkorps (NSFK) instructor. The NSFK was a paramilitary organisation of the Nazi Party that was founded on 15 April 1937.

Spitfire prototype K5054 after being brought up to Mk I standards and camouflaged in standard RAF day fighter colours.

Messerschmitt Bf 109 V1 Wk-Nr 758 performed its first flight on 28 May 1935 from Augsburg-Haunstetten airfield. At the controls was Messerschmitt's senior test pilot, Hans-Dietrich 'Bubi' Knoetzsch.

Bristol Type 142 K-7557 was the development aircraft for the Blenheim.

The Air Ministry's Air Council oversaw the operations of the RAF, the latter's Chief of the Air Staff reporting directly to this august body of men. This photograph was taken in July 1940.

Fairey Battle Is of No 63 Squadron prior to flying a training mission from RAF Upwood in September 1937.

POSITION OF AIRCRAFT

AIRCRAFT	STAGES OUTSTANDING	STAGE SUBMITTED TO INSPECTION	STAGE CLEARED A.I.D.

'The balloon goes up at 11.15hrs. That's official'

JOHN SIMPSON No 43 SQN

Previous: Blenheim I production line at Bristol's Filton works in April 1939.

Airmen of No 139 Squadron march past their Blenheim Is and two Battle Is in 1938 at RAF Halton.

These Spitfire Is were amongst the first batch of 310 fighters ordered (308 delivered) by the Air Ministry and built by Supermarine at its Woolston plant between May 1938 and September 1939.

Blitzkrieg

On 1 September 1939, 56 German divisions crossed the Polish border under the cover of darkness. The Anglo-French governments, despite their alliance with Poland, failed to immediately declare war. Instead, Paris and London expressed their willingness to negotiate should Hitler withdraw his forces from Poland. However, by the morning of 3 September it was obvious that war with Germany could no longer be avoided. At 11.15hrs, a reluctant Prime Minister Neville Chamberlain addressed the nation over the radio, officially announcing that Britain was at war with Germany.

Amongst those listening intently to his broadcast was future ace Flt Lt Peter Townsend of No 43 Squadron based at Tangmere:

'I was lying beside my Hurricane watching flaky white clouds drift across a blue sky, while hovering larks shrilled and voices came to me from pilots and groundcrew also lying beside their dispersed aircraft. Never in my life had I experienced so peaceful a scene.

'At 11.00hrs squadron adjutant John Simpson walked into the hangar and said, "The balloon goes up at 11.15hrs. That's official."

'We all forgathered in the mess where we had listened to Hitler's shrieking voice just over a year ago. Our station commander, Fred Sowrey, looked grave. But the presence of this veteran was reassuring for us who did not know war. Twenty-three years earlier to the very day, Fred Sowrey had been on patrol with Lt Leefe Robinson when Robinson sent a Zeppelin crashing in flames near London. Then Zeppelin L32 had fallen to Sowrey's guns, and in May 1918 he was in at the kill of the last German raider to crash on English soil. This veteran of the first generation of airmen was about to see the horror of the second attempt by the Germans to reduce England to her knees by bombing. He steadied us in our ardour to "get at the Hun". He told us, "Don't think a fighter pilot's life is one of endless flying and glory. You will spend nine-tenths of your time sitting on your backsides waiting".

'Macey and Hoskins, two imperturbables in white jackets, served us each a mug of bitter. The swing door by which they entered the ante-room seemed to creak louder as the silence grew and the fateful hour approached.

'Then suddenly the radio came alive and the sombre, leaden tones of Prime Minister Neville Chamberlain fell on the silence of the ante-room. "It is a sad day for all of us. Every aim for which I have worked, everything I had hoped for, all the principles in which I believed have fallen down in ruin. I hope to live long enough to see the day when Hitlerism will be destroyed and a free Europe will exist again."

'Chamberlain would never live to see that day. Neither would most of us who listened to him. The ebullient Caesar Hull jumped from one foot to another exclaiming "Wizard!", and turning to John Simpson, "Never mind, John, you'll be killed early on." And he punched him in the back and laughed.

'John, however, would come through (like me) by pure luck. But not Caesar, nor Wilkinson, nor "Womb" Woods-Scawen in A Flight. Nor "Tiger" Folkes, Eddy Edmonds, Pat Christie or Joe Sullivan in B Flight. Within 12 months or so these valiant young men who cared for nothing more than the joy of flying would die in the fight to destroy Hitlerism. Not counting the wounded and the burnt, escape was a one-in-five chance.

'But no such thoughts troubled us then. As John wrote, "It's the war we've been expecting, so we can't grumble".'

At RAF Fighter Command airfields across the country units sprang into action. At Biggin Hill, No 79 Squadron was ordered to scramble. Amongst those pilots racing to their Hurricanes was South African Flg Off Edward Morris, who later became an ace:

'Immediately after the Prime Minister's announcement we were ordered to Cockpit Readiness. When we had strapped in and switched on the R/T we were ordered to start engines and Stand By. We sat for what seemed ages with the engines getting hotter all the time until the Squadron Commander called Operations and told them either we had to take off or close down the engines before they all boiled. Rather reluctantly they agreed to stopping our engines, but we had to remain at Cockpit Readiness.'

It would be many months before No 79 Squadron, or any other fighter squadron in No 11 Group in southeast England for that matter, would be scrambled to intercept German aircraft.

This was certainly not the case some 900 miles to the northeast, as the Polish Air Force fought for its very survival against overwhelming odds. Nearly 2,000 modern fighters, medium bombers and dive-bombers had been committed to 'Case White', as the Defensive War in

Poland was codenamed by the Wehrmacht. The principal Polish fighter was the PZL P.11, which, although poorly armed and slower than most German types it met in combat, performed surprisingly well. Only 12 Polish fighter pilots were killed in action and seven posted missing in action during the four-week campaign, and in turn they accounted for 116 German aircraft. Overall, the Luftwaffe lost 285 aeroplanes (with a further 279 being severely damaged). Polish Air Force losses were remarkably similar, with 264 aircraft being destroyed and 116 fleeing to Romania. Around 100,000 soldiers, sailors and airmen fled Poland initially for France, before heading to Britain in June 1940 to fight on as Free Poles – 146 would take part in the Battle of Britain. The USSR invaded Poland from the east on 17 September and Warsaw finally fell 10 days later.

Instead of turning his attention to the West, Hitler chose to make good his losses in Poland and delay any attack until the spring of 1940. The eight months of relative peace that followed the Polish campaign were dubbed 'The Bore War' by the British public, Winston Churchill christening it the 'sinister trance'. Hitler had in fact hoped to launch his offensive in the West as soon as possible, ordering his army chiefs to devise plans for an all-out assault. The weather had intervened, however, halting the plans. Hitler was not overly concerned, as the proposals initially presented to him lacked imagination in his view. The long, unusually cold winter of 1939-40 gave some of his more gifted generals more time to plan. In February 1940 Generalleutnant Erich von Manstein briefed the Führer on his bold strategy for a sickle-cut manoeuvre through the Belgian Ardennes to the North Sea. Hitler immediately approved the plan, with a launch date set for May once the spring had arrived.

In the West, this period of 'Phoney War' had allowed the British government to bolster France's defences through mobilisation of the British Expeditionary Force (BEF) in September 1939. It was supported by an air component that included two Hurricane-equipped fighter units, Nos 85 and 87 Squadrons. A small bomber fleet of Battles and Blenheims, dubbed the Advanced Air Striking Force, was also transferred to France. Its dedicated fighter escort was provided by Hurricanes of Nos 1 and 73 Squadrons.

From the first deployment in September 1939 until the following spring, events on the frontline in the West were relatively quiet for the RAF. This was to Air Chief Marshal Sir Hugh Dowding's great relief, as the Commander-in-Chief of Fighter Command had been vehemently opposed to even sending four squadrons of his precious fighters to France when Britain's own defences were in such a parlous state. He would duly wage an uphill battle with Whitehall over the next eight months to 'protect' his carefully husbanded fighter units from the French campaign.

Throughout the autumn and winter of 1939 and during the early months of 1940, activity on the Western Front was limited to the reconnaissance flights by either side, which occasionally resulted in aerial action taking place. RAF and Armeé de l'Air fighters intercepted high-flying Luftwaffe Heinkel He 111s and Dornier Do 17s as they probed Allied defences on the French-German border. Occasionally, Messerschmitt Bf 109s would also be encountered, as they provided fighter escort for the vulnerable reconnaissance aircraft. With an improvement in the weather, the tempo of aerial fighting increased in March 1940 to the point where, on the 26th, the RAF recognised its first ace when New Zealander Flg Off E. K. 'Cobber' Kain of No 73 Squadron claimed his fifth victory. He related his experiences during this historic mission to Noel Monks, a correspondent with the 'Daily Mail':

'I shouted into my microphone "Messerschmitts ahead. Let's go!" The Messerschmitts came at us in twos, trying to get on our tails, but it ended up with us on their tails. I got one right in my sights and gave him a full burst. Down he went in flames. I then noticed five more Messerschmitts working around behind me, so I turned hard right and took a sight on the nearest one. I fired a quick burst at the aircraft before it dived away, then made three deflection shots at another enemy aircraft that slowly turned ahead of me, before getting directly behind it and giving it a longer burst. He gave me a bit of a chase but I got him. The enemy aircraft turned on its starboard side and dived vertically towards earth.

'By then the sky was full of aircraft darting in different directions. I could see only swastikas flashing by. After getting my second Messerschmitt I let down my guard for just a moment to look for my two wingmen. I breathed deeply then yoicks! The hood over the cockpit was ripped off. A Messerschmitt cannon had let go at me. My engine caught fire as the gravity tank had also been hit. Flames and oil came into the cockpit and I found myself in a steep dive from 24,000ft. I passed out for a few seconds, then, coming to, I bent forward and tried,

British Prime Minister Winston Churchill soon became the living embodiment of the national spirit of defiance during the summer of 1940.

Hitler addresses the Reichstag at the Kroll Opera House in Berlin on 19 July 1940, delivering his self-titled 'Last Appeal to Reason' speech to the British government and the British people.

Flg Off E. K. 'Cobber' Kain

unsuccessfully, to turn off the petrol to the engine, scorching my face. I then pulled back on the stick and managed to come out of the dive. I quickly undid my straps, rolled over and slipped from the cockpit. The rush of cold air felt good on my face.

'I couldn't pull the rip-cord to release the parachute because my flying gloves were covered in oil. Tearing off a glove, I finally tugged the rip-cord at 10,000ft and soon found myself hanging sideways from the parachute – my left-shoulder strap had come loose. Remembering I was somewhere near the German border, I pulled on a shroud to spill air out of the canopy, pushing me to the south. I came down with a wallop in no-man's-land. Picking myself up, I ran like the devil to a small wood and from there I could see a village. I decided not to make for it, but to walk towards the sun, going cautiously. A minute or two later a French officer came running up and challenged at the point of a pistol, asking me my nationality.'

Initially receiving treatment for a bullet wound in the hand by a French doctor, 'Cobber' Kain was soon returned to his squadron. Here, he received treatment for shrapnel wounds, as well as the attention of the press. On the evening of 28 March 1940 the awarding of the Distinguished Flying Cross to Flg Off E. J. Kain was announced.

This period of relative inactivity in the West came to an end on 10 May 1940 when the Germans launched Operation 'Fall Gelb' (Case Yellow), based on Generalleutnant von Manstein's plan. The latter called for armoured units to push through the Ardennes and then along the Somme valley to cut off and surround Allied units that had quickly advanced into Belgium in an attempt to form a defensive chain from the Meuse to Antwerp. When British and French forces were pushed back to the sea by the highly mobile German blitzkrieg operation, the British government successfully evacuated the BEF, as well as a handful of French divisions, from Dunkirk in Operation 'Dynamo'.

Going into 'Fall Gelb', the Luftwaffe had amassed a force of 3,500 modern aircraft, including two air fleets equipped with 1,300 twin-engined bombers, 380 dive-bombers (Ju 87s and Hs 123s), 860 Bf 109s and 350 Bf 110s. They would be supporting 136 Wehrmacht divisions totalling some two million men. The combined British, French, Belgian and Dutch armies opposing them were actually greater in number in terms of men and materiel, but the Wehrmacht was better equipped, far more mobile, fielded more modern tanks and artillery, had better leadership and enjoyed the advantage of surprise. The Luftwaffe's primary task was to provide close air support for troops and tanks on the ground, with its Ju 87s, He 111s, Ju 88s and Do 17s being in the vanguard of such missions.

By May 1940, the Luftwaffe was the best trained, most modern and battle-hardened air force in the world. Benefitting from having no constricting central doctrine, other than it was to be used generally to support national strategy, the Luftwaffe had already shown in Poland that it could conduct tactical and strategic bombing effectively. Flexibility proved to be the Luftwaffe's primary strength during the Blitzkrieg of 1940, for while Allied air forces were tied to supporting the French and British armies in the field, the Luftwaffe employed its fighters, bombers and support types (troop transports and gliders) as the situation demanded in a very fluid frontline. This meant that units could operate as a Panzer spearhead on one mission, then switch to performing strategic or tactical bombing on the next. During the course of a single day, fighters could be escorting medium bombers attacking key bridges or defensive positions in the morning and then be given licence to perform a freie jagd (free hunt) in search of enemy fighters or targets on the ground to strafe in the afternoon.

During one such freie jagd on 15 May, Oberleutnant Hans von Hahn, Staffelkapitän of 8./JG 53 and a future 31-victory ace, engaged RAF Hurricanes for the first time during the Battle of France (he had claimed one shot down some five months earlier during the Phoney War):

'The first enemy aircraft we encountered were RAF Hurricanes and I was able to claim my second victory against one of them. On that day we were flying with "Vati" [Hauptman Werner Mölders, Gruppenkommandeur of III./JG 53] again. At first we didn't see any enemy aircraft, but before the Maas the Kommandeur suddenly said over the radio, "Look out – Stukas!" When we got nearer, we discovered that the aircraft carried roundels – enemy roundels. Belgians [they were in fact RAF Hurricanes, as all the Belgian Air Force examples had been lost in the first 48 hours of the Blitzkrieg]. Everything was chaotic. We did not really attempt to fight, but I managed to get into a favourable position behind a brown and green camouflaged enemy aeroplane. The pilot went into a dive and began evasive manoeuvres, always flying in a westerly direction. However, I managed to keep my attacking position and opened fire. By my third burst he only had half his tail left. Bits of his wings flew towards me. His right wing was shredded. Finally, he disappeared behind a wood, and I thought "he's had it".'

The RAF had doubled the number of Hurricane squadrons it had in France within hours of the German invasion of the Low Countries and the eight units permanently based on the continent were reinforced by No 11 Group squadrons flying patrols from their English bases. Calls for yet more reinforcements saw pilots from home-based squadrons sent to units in France, but the losses continued to mount at an alarming rate. So far only Hurricanes had been committed to the Battle of France, prompting many to ask 'where are the Spitfires' – they would at last commence operations off the French coast on 16 May, but none would ever be based in France, primarily because Air Vice Marshal Dowding fought vehemently to keep them in Britain.

As a direct result of Dowding's intervention, plans to send more squadrons to France were immediately put on hold. However, pilots and aircraft continued to be despatched across the Channel on a piecemeal basis. 'Replacements came for the aeroplanes we lost in France and we lost them too, and more replacements came and we lost them as well', recalled Sqn Ldr Teddy Donaldson, CO of No 151 Squadron. 'I think we must have lost dozens of aeroplanes in our squadron alone in France – burnt out, bombed or shot down. We were in an awful shape by the time we finally got pulled back to England.'

What was left of the BEF's Air Component withdrew back to airfields in England between 19 and 21 May. With the evacuation of the Air Component, only the AASF squadrons – retreating to the south and west – remained in France. However, RAF fighters continued to be committed to the campaign from bases in England as the retreating BEF fell back to Dunkirk.

On 23 May Göring told Milch that he had 'managed to talk the Führer round to halting the Army. The Luftwaffe is to wipe out the British on the beaches'. Hitler did indeed order the Panzer divisions to halt the following day, but this was almost certainly because there was concern by commanders in the field that the armoured divisions might struggle to penetrate the now-flooded lowlands of Flanders. The divisions' long logistical tail was now also vulnerable to counter-attack.

That same day (24 May) Spitfires clashed with Bf 109Es, having encountered the German fighter for the very first time just 24 hours earlier. Squadrons flying the RAF's premier fighter had now been ordered to provide cover and support for Allied forces withdrawing to Dunkirk from the Low Countries, which brought them into direct contact with the Bf 109.

Amongst the units involved was No 54 Squadron, whose Johnny Allen (later to be killed in action by Adolf Galland – the first Spitfire downed by the German ace) and Al Deere engaged Bf 109Es from I./JG 27 over Calais-Marck airfield. Deere later recalled:

'This was my first real combat, and the first recorded combat of a Spitfire with a Bf 109. My abiding memory was the thrill of the action – there was no sense of danger at that early stage in the war. So much so that I stayed behind the second of the two Bf 109s that I encountered after I had run out of ammunition just to see if I could do so. I only broke off when petrol became a factor. My prolonged fight with this Bf 109 allowed me to assess the relative performance of the two aircraft.

'In early engagements between the Hurricane and Bf 109 in France, the speed and climb of the latter had become legendary and were claimed by many to be far superior to that of the Spitfire. I was able to refute this and indeed was confident that, except in a dive, the Spitfire was superior in most other fields and was vastly more manoeuvrable. My superior rate of climb was, however, due mostly to the type of Spitfire with which my squadron was equipped. We had the first Rotol constant-speed aircrews on which we had had been doing trials when the fighting started. Other Spitfires were, at that stage, using a two-speed airscrew (either fully fine pitch or fully course), which meant they lost performance in a climb. The constant-speed unit changed its pitch as the engine revs went up.

'There was a great deal of scepticism about my claim that the Spitfire was the superior fighter, but the big thing for me was that we shouldn't have any fear of the Bf 109 in combat.'

A number of Spitfire units suffered significant losses on 24 May, however, including No 92 Squadron, flying from Hornchurch. It had encountered Bf 109s and Bf 110s the previous day and although a handful of German aircraft had been destroyed by the unit, two pilots had been killed, two captured (including the CO, Sqn Ldr Roger Bushell) and one wounded. No 92 Squadron had been helping to defend Calais the previous day and on the 24th it managed to scrape together eight Spitfires for a morning patrol along the French coast from Boulogne up to Dunkirk. Leading the unit was future high-scoring ace Flt Lt Bob Stanford Tuck.

'*The sky was full of aircraft darting in different directions. I could see only swastikas flashing by*'

EDGAR 'COBBER' KAIN No 73 SQN

In Tuck's biography 'Fly For Your Life', author Larry Forrester describes the mission:

'They went up and down their "beat" twice, and then they spotted a formation of 20 Dornier 17s at about 12,000ft, far inland. Behind the bombers and about 7,000ft higher – 4,000ft above the Spits – gleamed a protective arrowhead of Messerschmitt 110s. Tuck knew he had to ignore the fighters and try to break up the Dornier formation before they could start their bombing run.

'"Buster!"

'The eight pilots pushed their throttles forward through the emergency seals to full power and the Spitfires slashed inland in a shallow curving dive. Tuck meant to bring them round in a wide half-circle on the tails of the bomber stream, but was prepared to change direction and risk a head-on or beam attack if the escorting 110s dropped down to intercept.

'A wonderful stroke of luck then relieved him of this worry. As he glanced again at the high wedge of fighters he saw a squadron of Hurricanes hurtling almost vertically down out of the remote blue, quick as minnows, and in a perfect "bounce". In mere seconds the Messerschmitt pack was shattered into writhing fragments, completely taken up with the business of its own survival. Now the Dorniers would have to look out for themselves.

'The bombers were flying in wide, flat "vics" of three. As the Spits came down on their tails they were in a gentle turn to starboard, lining up to start their bombing run. Tony Bartley's section, on the inside of the Spitfire's curving dive, got within range before Tuck's flight. As Bob recalls it, "Tony did a rather extraordinary thing. He went down the starboard side of the stream, shooting them up one wing, and I distinctly saw him leapfrog over one 'vic', under the next, then up over the third – and so on. He did the whole side of the formation like that, and he tumbled at least one – maybe two – as flamers during that single pass. It was just about the cheekiest bit of flying I'd ever seen. The chaps in his section tried to follow, but they managed only one or two of the 'jumps'. Tony made every one".'

According to Tuck, the Do 17 gunners put up a spirited defence, 'blazing defiance' and 'laying on a heavy crossfire'. They succeeded in hitting one of the Spitfires in Tony Bartley's section, P9374, flown by Flg Off Peter Cazenove. He made a wheels-up landing on the beach at Calais and was subsequently captured, while his Spitfire was slowly swallowed by the tides.

Young men and boys crowd around an RAF recruiting van at the very last Hendon Empire Air Day on 20 May 1939.

Hurricanes dominate a 1940-issue recruitment poster for the RAF, which has been pinned to the door of a hastily set up recruiting centre.

A Ju 87B drops a single SC 250 and four SC 50 bombs during a mission in the summer of 1940.

Oblt Josef Fözö of 2./JG 71 is helped on with his parachute by the unit's Schwarzemanner (black men), as Luftwaffe groundcrew were referred to due to the colour of their overalls. Fözö was credited with 10 victories during the Battle of Britain and survived the war with 23 kills from 517 sorties.

'We shall fight with growing confidence and growing strength in the air, we shall defend our Island, whatever the cost may be'

WINSTON CHURCHILL

A flight of Spitfires Is from Hornchurch-based No 65 Squadron fly in formation in the spring of 1939, led by future ace Flg Off Bob Stanford Tuck.

No 92 Squadron Spitfire I P9374 was force-landed on the beach at Calais by Flg Off Peter Cazenove on 24 May 1940 after it had been hit by return fire from a Do 17 of I./KG 77. Cazenove was captured and the aircraft became something of a tourist attraction for German soldiers during the summer of 1940. It would remain buried on the beach until recovered in 1981 and eventually restored to airworthiness (right).

Groundcrew check the flaps of a Do 17Z for ice prior to a mission on a cold, crisp day during the bitter winter of 1939-40.

Male and female engineers complete the installation of the actuating gear for a VDM propeller that has been fitted to a wingless Bf 109E.

A Bf 109E-1 of 1.IJG 26 about to have its guns harmonised in the firing pit at Diepholz, in February 1940.

No 85 Squadron's Flt Lt 'Dickie' Lee and Plt Off Albert Lewis, who between them claimed at least 15 victories during the Blitzkrieg. Lee went missing in action on 18 August 1940 and Lewis was badly burned and baled out of a Hurricane on 28 September 1940.

With the engine of his weather-beaten Battle I already running, the pilot 'mounts up' at an airfield in France on 1 May 1940.

Virtually all aircraft maintenance undertaken by the RAF in France in 1939-40 took place in the open, as this No 1 Squadron Hurricane I at Vassincourt clearly shows.

ROLLS-ROYCE

Armourers load 0.303in rounds into belts for fitment into the magazines of No 85 Squadron Hurricanes at Lille-Seclin, spring of 1940.

Pilots of No 87 Squadron at Lille-Seclin gather round a fuselage panel of a Heinkel He 111 claimed during the Battle of France.

During the Battle of France, No 1 Squadron was credited with 63 aerial victories and 11 probables for the loss of two pilots killed, one captured and four wounded. The officers pose outside their hotel (the 'Marie') at Neuville in early 1940. Left to right: Plt Off Billy Drake, Flg Offs Les Clisby and 'Lorry' Lorimer (both killed in action on 14 May 1940), Flt Lt 'Prosser' Hanks, Plt Off 'Boy' Mould, Sqn Ldr 'Bull' Halahan, Lt Jean 'Moses' Demozay (French liaison officer), Flt Lt 'Johnny' Walker, 'Doc' Brown (squadron medical officer), Flg Offs Paul Richey and 'Killy' Kilmartin, Plt Off 'Stratters' Stratton and Flg Off 'Pussy' Palmer. Both Walker and Palmer are wearing carpet slippers!

Plt Off Billy Drake claimed three confirmed and two unconfirmed victories prior to being wounded and forced to bale out of his Hurricane on 13 May 1940 after being attacked by Bf 110s.

Six Hurricane Is of Reims-based No 73 Squadron hold station in loose line abreast on 19 April 1940.

Dashing over the muddy expanses of Vassincourt towards their aircraft, No 1 Squadron pilots perform a mock scramble – note the smile on Plt Off 'Lorry' Lorimer's face – in early 1940.

German bombers could absorb a lot of punishment as most Allied fighters at the start of the war were armed exclusively with rifle-calibre machine guns, rather than hard-hitting cannon. French and RAF airmen can be seen examining a shot-up, but essentially intact, He 111P that came down on French soil during the final weeks of the Phoney War.

One of the Hurricane Is that No 73 Squadron flew in 1940 was P3351, which later served with the Soviet Red Air Force and was eventually shot down near Murmansk during the winter of 1943-44. Recovered in 1992, the fighter was restored to airworthiness in 2000.

The original, unrestored, fuselage step used by pilots when climbing into the cockpit of Hurricane I P3351. The imprint of their boots has been worn into the aluminium plate that wraps around the wooden step.

GEOFFREY ALLARD

Pilot Officer

Yorkshireman Geoffrey 'Sammy' Allard was a Halton 'Brat', having joined the RAF in September 1929. He applied for pilot training in 1936 and joined No 87 Squadron at Debden as a sergeant pilot in October of the following year. Switching to No 85 Squadron when it reformed with Gladiators at Debden in June 1938, Allard accompanied the unit to France in September 1939. During the hectic and chaotic days of the May 1940 Blitzkrieg, Allard was reported to have claimed 10 victories in seven days, before being posted home for a rest. Awarded a DFM on 31 May and also commissioned as a pilot officer, Allard claimed a further nine and three shared destroyed during the Battle of Britain prior to No 85 Squadron being posted out of the frontline to No 13 Group. Having survived the intense combat of the Battles of France and Britain, Allard was killed in a flying accident at the controls of a Havoc intruder on 13 March 1941. By the time of his death he had claimed 19 and five shared victories.

Sgt 'Sammy' Allard of No 85 Squadron downs an He IIIH of III./KG I during the afternoon of 10 May 1940. He claimed three Heinkel bombers destroyed on this date.

'*Saw a He 111 on my left. Climbed into sun to 8,000ft and aligned quarter attacks – each time I closed to within 50 yards. Enemy aircraft dived into ground in flames one mile off Condcourt [Contescourt]. Nothing of enemy aircraft remains*'

GEOFFREY ALLARD

Dunkirk

During the early evening of 26 May 1940, the order was given to commence the evacuation of the BEF and French troops from the beaches of Dunkirk. The operation was codenamed 'Dynamo'. Having staged a fighting retreat to the small fishing port on the north coast of France, the BEF was now reliant on the Royal Navy to get as many men back to England as it could. Vice-Admiral Bertram Ramsey masterminded 'Dynamo' from a bunker deep within the Dover cliffs, his carefully planned perfectly executed operation extracting 198,229 British soldiers and 139,997 French troops between 27 May and the early hours of 4 June.

Throughout the evacuation the naval vessels offshore and the troops waiting patiently on the beaches were attacked by the Luftwaffe, which threw everything it had at Dunkirk. It was Fighter Command's job to prevent the bombers from getting through, No 11 Group being specifically tasked with this mission due to its close proximity to the evacuation beaches. Its perceived performance during 'Dynamo' did little to enhance the reputation of the RAF, as few on the ground coming under seemingly constant aerial attack realised how hard pilots fought to protect those on the beaches below. One of the soldiers was Sgt Maj Martin McLane of C Company, 2nd Battalion, Durham Light Infantry, whose view on the part played by the RAF in 'Dynamo' was shared by the vast majority of the troops plucked from the beaches:

'The RAF did a very poor job of defending us. The German troops were working in close co-operation with their aircraft. When they wanted support, they called in their dive-bombers and their fighters, who strafed and bombed us to clear the way. And what support did we have? We had no damn thing at all. Not a bloody thing. We were just left to God and good neighbours.'

Although soldiers like Sgt Maj McLane saw bombers pounding them from below the cloud and smoke that often blanketed the beaches, these same troops did not see the bloody battles raging higher in the air as Fighter Command fought to prevent the Luftwaffe from reaching Dunkirk. However, Fighter Command was incapable of staging continuous patrols over the evacuation area to protect all of the soldiers all of the time because it simply had too few aircraft. Air Vice-Marshal Keith Park, who led No 11 Group, had only 200 aeroplanes to oppose a Luftwaffe force of 350 bombers and 550 fighters.

Despite being outnumbered, the British pilots endured an exhausting number of patrols throughout the evacuation period, fighters being sent north of the beaches in an effort to intercept the bomber fleets before they could make their attacks. They were hampered by the limited time that patrols could spend over the French coast, as it took more than 20 minutes to reach Dunkirk from Biggin Hill and Kenley, giving pilots just 30 minutes on patrol. If enemy aircraft were engaged, the violent manoeuvring associated with dogfighting meant that aircraft had to return early due to excessive fuel consumption. It came as no surprise, therefore, that the evacuees only ever seemed to see German aeroplanes in the sky above them. No 19 Squadron was one of the Fighter Command unit's heavily committed to 'Dynamo', its future ranking ace of 1940, Flt Sgt George Unwin, having sympathy with the BEF's plight on the ground – and their grievances with the RAF:

'They were on the beaches or damned near the beaches. Now very little fighting took place over the beaches. What we tried to do was to stop the bombers, catch the bombers before they reached the beaches. There was no point in stopping them when they were over the beaches, and so what fighting did go on, most of it would be inland.

'Once you had got rid of your ammunition you simply went home for more ammunition and to refuel. When you arrived there would be Germans there, always, because they had such a very short distance to come and they had far more aircraft than we had. So the target was there when we arrived so we probably went over, not fighting for more than five minutes, and then off we went back home. I can understand our soldiers thinking that they were all on their own, but they were quite wrong, quite wrong. In fact if we hadn't been there I don't think many of them would have got out.'

No 11 Group would fly a total of 2,739 sorties over Dunkirk, fighting what would prove to be the RAF's costliest battle of the French campaign. It lost 106 fighters and had 56 Spitfire and Hurricane pilots killed and eight captured. In return they claimed 390 German aircraft destroyed (132 were actually downed). Many of the squadrons involved in 'Dynamo' were experiencing combat for the first time, as the combat-weary Hurricane squadrons pulled out of France had been posted to northern England to rest and recuperate. These untried

squadrons flew into action as they had been taught to in peacetime – in rigid formations.

The Spitfires and Hurricanes flown by Fighter Command were armed exclusively with rifle-calibre 0.303in machine guns at this time and their weight of fire was deemed to be insufficient to bring down bombers flying in tight, massed formations when attacking independently of one another. The AFDE therefore decided that the only way to solve this problem was to mass fighters in close formation so as to bring a large number of guns to bear. Pilots in frontline fighter units were well drilled in formation flying, so a series of six basic patterns known as Fighting Area Attacks were duly formulated and published in the RAF Manual of Air Tactics, published in 1938. These were at the heart of standard squadron air drills pre-war, as Al Deere of No 54 Squadron recalled:

'The majority of our training in a pre-war fighter squadron was directed at achieving perfection in formation, with a view to ensuring the success of the flight and the squadron attacks we so assiduously practised. The order to attack was always preceded by the flight commander designating the number of the attack, such as "Fighting Area Attack No 5 – Go". These attacks provided wonderful training for formation drill, but were worthless when related to effective shooting. There was never sufficient time to get one's sights on the target, the business of keeping station being the prime requirement.'

The standard RAF fighter formation at the time was the V-shaped 'vic' of three aircraft. A squadron of 12 aircraft would be split into two flights, A and B, and these were in turn made up of two sections of three fighters. When in full-strength Battle Formation, all 12 aircraft would be tightly grouped together in four sections of three fighters. Leading the 'vic' would be the squadron CO or senior flight commander, with succeeding 'Vs' following in close line astern. Once bombers had been spotted, the commander would position his formation in behind them and then lead the attack in section after section.

Such attacks would have worked well against German bombers had it not been for the presence of agile escort fighters sweeping the skies ahead of them. Luftwaffe tactics were far more flexible in nature and centred on smaller formations engaging other fighters, rather than just bombers. As Fighter Command quickly find out to its cost, Fighting Area Attacks were useless against small, nimble formations of high performance fighters such as the Bf 109E. Indeed, upon seeing British fighters flying into combat in tight neat rows of three, German pilots quickly dubbed the 'vics' 'Idiotenreihen' (rows of idiots).

Those pilots that survived their initial encounters with the enemy soon came to realise that a successful combat formation had to be able to manoeuvre while maintaining cohesion. Pilots also had to be able to cover each other's blind areas so as to prevent surprise attacks on the formation. Finally, individual members of the formation had to be able to support each other should they come under attack.

However, over Dunkirk, virtually all Fighter Command units committed to 'Dynamo' employed Fighting Area Attacks. No 19 Squadron, which had temporarily moved from its Duxford home to Hornchurch so as to be closer to the French coast, went into action for the first time on 26 May in its tight formations, which, according to Flt Sgt George Unwin, were 'better suited for a Hendon air display. You went in, in formation, in line astern threes, and you picked off your target, which was supposed to be only a bomber – that was the foreseen enemy. So you went in formation attacking a formation of bombers, which flew straight and level and didn't try to evade you. This was the plan and of course the first lot we saw were a load of Junkers 87s. We went in in Fighting Area Attack No 1 and of course we were going about twice as fast as they were and rapidly overhauled them. Throttling back, we tried to get a sight of them, forgetting all about the fact that there might be escorts, and their escorts came down and clobbered us. The front three, the CO and his two wingmen, were shot down. One was killed, another died of his wounds two days later and the CO spent the rest of the war in a prison camp.'

As with the RAF units that had been based in France with the BEF and AASF, the No 11 Group squadrons were operating without the benefit of radar. They were also at the limit of their range, with the ever-present worry of having to ditch in the Channel once their fuel was exhausted. Nevertheless, they continued to perform the task they had been given until the last evacuation vessels left Dunkirk in the early hours of 4 June.

Another pilot making his combat debut during 'Dynamo' was 19-year-old Yorkshireman Plt Off Hugh Dundas of No 616 Squadron, who described what he saw when patrolling off the French coast:

'There was this enormous great pall of smoke, which was rising up from, I think, some of the oil tanks that had been set on fire – a huge black pillar of smoke that came up and spread out and then levelled off and went down the Channel for a distance of 75 to 100 miles. Underneath that there was a lot of haze and general mayhem. It was altogether a very confusing scene due to the cloud and smoke. I think that's one of the reasons why perhaps the army had the impression that the RAF wasn't there half the time, because there was no control. We were outside the range of our own radar. We just had to go in there. All the time one was playing a game of blind man's bluff. Very often one wasn't at the right height. Of course, the Germans were operating from fields that were comparatively close. They could come in and out very quickly. There was an awful lot of luck as to whether one was in the right place at the right time.'

Although the bulk of the BEF had been rescued at Dunkirk, it had been forced to leave behind almost 500 tanks, 38,000 vehicles, 1,000 heavy guns and tons of ammunition. The British Army was in no fit state to fight any further battles for the time being. The frontline defence of Britain would have to be provided by Fighter Command, a point that combat-weary pilots like Plt Off Roland Beamont of No 87 Squadron were fully aware of:

'We who'd been in the French battle came home convinced that there was only one thing that was going to stop the enemy crossing the Channel and that would be us. We could see that coming all the way through the summer of 1940. By July and August it was building up to a fury. We knew absolutely that there was just one frontline holding. It had to be us that did it.'

Although the bulk of the BEF had been evacuated through Dunkirk, a large number of British troops remained in France. They retreated in good order to western ports for evacuation, their progress being covered by three AASF Hurricane squadrons still on the continent and UK-based fighters. Nos 17 and 242 Squadrons also briefly joined the AASF on 7 June, but all remaining Hurricanes in France had been withdrawn to England by the 18th, when No 73 Squadron returned to Tangmere from Nantes. By 22 June, RAF losses in the West had reached 959 aircraft of all types, including 66 during the failed defence of Norway. Of this total, 509 were fighters, and 435 of Fighter Command's pilots had been listed as killed, missing or captured. Just 66 of the hundreds of Hurricanes sent to France made the return journey and many of these aircraft were so badly damaged that they were scrapped where they sat at airfields along the south coast of England. In early June Fighter Command had an operational strength of just 331 single-engined

fighters. However, the Luftwaffe had lost 247 of its Bf 109s and 108 Bf 110s during the campaign in France.

On 18 June Prime Minister Winston Churchill, using all his skills as an orator, made one of his legendary speeches to the nation in an attempt to galvanise the British population for what lay ahead:

'What General Weygand called the Battle of France is over. I expect that the Battle of Britain is about to begin. The whole fury and might of the enemy must very soon be turned on us. Hitler knows that he will have to break us in this island or lose the war. If we can stand up to him, all Europe may be free and the life of the world may move forward into broad sunlit uplands. But if we fail, then the whole world, including the United States, including all that we have known and cared for, will sink into the abyss of a new Dark Age, made more sinister and perhaps more protracted by the lights of perverted science. Let us therefore brace ourselves to our duties, and bear ourselves that, if the British Empire and its Commonwealth last for a thousand years, men will say, "This was their finest hour".'

Air Chief Marshal Dowding, whose Fighter Command would be responsible for the defence of Britain, was more economical in his response to France's surrender four days after Churchill's speech:

'Thank God we are now alone.'

'What General Weygand called the Battle of France is over.
I expect that the Battle of Britain is about to begin.
The whole fury and might of the enemy must very soon be turned on us.
Hitler knows that he will have to break us in this island
or lose the war'

WINSTON CHURCHILL

No 19 Squadron's CO, Sqn Ldr Geoffrey Stephenson, force-landed his Spitfire I, N3200, on the beach at Sangatte, near Dunkirk. The fighter remained buried in the sand until recovered in the mid-1980s and subsequently restored to airworthiness.

ACES *in* ART

'Spitfires and 110s were slashing across and up and down, turning, writhing, rolling through the lethal latticework of tracer'

ROBERT STANFORD TUCK

ROBERT TUCK

Squadron Leader

'Bob' Tuck, from South London, joined the RAF on a short commission in September 1935 and was sent to No 65 Squadron at Hornchurch 11 months later after completing his flying training. The first pilot from his unit to fly the Spitfire, he was posted to No 92 Squadron as a flight commander at the beginning of May 1940. In the thick of the action during the latter stages of the Battle of France, Tuck soon 'made ace' and received a DFC in June for his successes in combat. Posted as CO to No 257 Squadron halfway through the Battle of Britain, he seamlessly switched from Spitfire to Hurricane and was one of the RAF's leading aces by the end of 1940. Following a brief rest in the autumn of 1941, Tuck returned to action as Wing Leader at Biggin Hill, only to be shot down by flak on 28 January 1942 – he spent the rest of the war as a PoW. By then he had claimed 27 and two shared destroyed, one and one shared unconfirmed destroyed and six probables.

Flying a sweep off Boulogne, Flt Lt 'Bob' Tuck of No 92 Squadron claimed three Bf 110s destroyed (and a Bf 109 unconfirmed) in his first day of combat on 23 May 1940.

Operation 'Seelöwe'

Although there is some contention as to whether the Germans ever seriously considered invading Britain following the fall of France, General Erhard Milch, State Secretary of the Air Ministry, did indeed propose immediate paratroop landings to seize key points in southeast England in the aftermath of the Dunkirk evacuation. This, he hoped, would pave the way for a full-scale invasion with whatever forces and transports could be assembled. However, it was not until 2 July 1940 that Hitler ordered the updating of the provisional invasion plans prepared before the war.

These had been hurriedly drawn up by Grand Admiral Erich Raeder, head of the Kriegsmarine, in 1939 primarily because he did not want to appear unprepared should Hitler or the Wehrmacht suddenly demand transport and protection for the invasion of Britain. Codenamed 'Study Red', Raeder's plan had outlined an invasion by just 7,500 troops on the south coast of England between Portland and the Isle of Wight. With victory in France, Raeder's Naval Staff modified his 'Study Red' into the new 'Study England', which would see a landing by 160,000 troops on a narrow front between Eastbourne and Dover. The Wehrmacht favoured a more ambitious undertaking that would have seen 250,000 men landing along a broad 100-mile front stretching from the Isle of Wight to Margate.

General Franz Halder, Chief of the Army General Staff, was given the job of amalgamating the Wehrmacht and Kriegsmarine proposals into a viable plan, which was duly presented to Hitler on 13 July as Operation 'Seelöwe' (Sealion). More than 260,000 men, 650 tanks, 34,200 vehicles, 62,000 horses and 26,000 bicycles would need to be transported across the Channel in two waves, with troops coming ashore in Kent, Sussex, Devon and Dorset. A further 25,000 airborne troops would also be involved. Halder was unimpressed by the criticism, noting in his diary on 6 August 1940: 'We have here the paradoxical situation where the navy is full of apprehension, the air force is very reluctant to tackle a mission which at the outset is exclusively its own, and OKW [Oberkommando der Wehrmacht, or Supreme Command of the Armed Forces] – which for once has a real combined operation to direct – just plays dead. The only driving force in the whole situation comes from us. But alone we can't swing it.'

Nevertheless, having studied 'Seelöwe' Hitler issued Führer-Direktiv No 16, which included the following statement: 'Since England, despite her hopeless military situation, shows no signs of coming to terms, I have decided to prepare a landing operation. The English air force must be so disabled in spirit as to be incapable of disrupting the crossing.'

The Channel ports soon began to fill with vessels for the invasion, which was scheduled to take place on 21 September (S-Day). Indeed, RAF reconnaissance aircraft routinely brought back photographs of the build-up. Despite British fears of an imminent invasion, the German High Command had in fact produced a makeshift invasion plan, having taken just two weeks to try and achieve what the Allies, with the D-Day landings, would subsequently spend two years preparing for.

The invasion's success hinged on the Luftwaffe attaining air superiority so that it could then defend the transports and barges from certain attack by the Royal Navy's powerful Home Fleet without interference from the RAF. Yet despite Göring's promise at the start of the offensive to wipe out Fighter Command, the Spitfire and Hurricane squadrons were very much in the ascendancy by mid-September, forcing 'Seelöwe' to be postponed on the 17th of that month.

Reichsmarschall Hermann Göring (sixth from the right), Commander-in-Chief of the Luftwaffe, stands amid his staff officers looking out across the English Channel at the white cliffs of Dover, 1 July 1940.

Hitler meets with his planning staff at Berghof, the Führer's mountain retreat, in 1940. On 17 July he was briefed here by his military chiefs on Operation 'Seelöwe' – the proposed invasion of Britain.

Invasion barges begin to mass in the harbour of Boulogne in July 1940. Photographs such as these, taken during highly dangerous daylight reconnaissance missions by unarmed RAF Spitfires, revealed to the British government just how serious the threat of invasion was in the summer of 1940.

A pilot from JG 26 enjoys a break from operations on a French Channel beach in June 1940.

The IRON EAGLE

Luftwaffe Aircraft and Strength

....

"They shall have Wars
and Pay for
Their Presumption"

King Henry the Sixth, Act IV, Scene I

William Shakespeare

The Iron Eagle

The German air arm mustering in large numbers on the Channel coast in preparation for the summer offensive against Britain, had only officially existed for five years. This was because the terms of the Treaty of Versailles, which came into effect in June 1919, limited Germany to tiny armed forces, with the air force and navy disbanded altogether. However, from the very beginning Germany was determined to rail against the restrictions imposed on it by the victorious Allies. Chief amongst the rebels was Colonel General Hans von Seeckt, head of the Reichswehr between 1919 and 1926. Having seen the effectiveness of German air power in World War 1, he was determined that a covert air force would continue to exist. Von Seeckt duly ensured that funds were allocated for a small, secret air arm comprised of 180 officers from the Deutsche Luftstreitkräfte to be retained as the nucleus of a new air force when the time was right. The men helped to staff a series of secret flying schools established in Russia as part of the Rapallo Treaty signed by the two countries in 1922.

German aircraft manufacturing also managed to keep going through the lean years of the 1920s by constructing civil aircraft for Deutsche Lufthansa. The latter was headed by Erhard Milch, a former air force officer and Nazi sympathiser, who encouraged companies such as Dornier, Heinkel and Junkers to develop airliners and fast mailplanes that could in fact be easily converted into bombers. Service with Deutsche Lufthansa also allowed a larger number of pilots to gain experience of long-range navigation in modern aircraft.

With the appointment of Hitler as Chancellor in 1933, Milch became State Secretary for Aviation in the Air Ministry under Hermann Göring. Although the latter was the public face of all things aviation in Germany from then on, it was Milch who effectively created the Air Ministry from scratch and laid the foundations for the new air force. He instigated a large-scale aircraft-building programme in January 1934 that saw no fewer than 4,021 aeroplanes ordered. Milch, an organisational genius, was so successful at his job that Hitler was able to announce the official existence of his Luftwaffe to the world on 27 March 1935.

When created, the Luftwaffe had a strength of 20,000 men and 1,888 aircraft. Although the Führer claimed parity with the RAF, this was a fallacy for most of the new air arm's aeroplanes were trainers or interim types. However, Milch's ambitious building programme would soon change this, as he intended to have sufficient aircraft available to equip six bomber, six reconnaissance and six fighter geschwader within 18 months.

The aircraft that would form the backbone of the Luftwaffe during the Battle of Britain were all evaluated at its flight-test centre at Rechlin during 1936. The Messerschmitt Bf 109, Junkers Ju 88, Dornier Do 17 and Heinkel He 111 would all outclass their British contemporaries in the lead up to World War 2, although the RAF's Spitfire and Hurricane would more than hold their own during the summer of 1940.

By 1936 the Luftwaffe had become a large and technically well-trained air force, lacking only in operational experience. This came in November of that year when the Condor Legion was formed to assist General Franco's Nationalist forces in the Spanish Civil War. Over the next two years the volunteer-manned Condor Legion would see considerable combat as Luftwaffe pilots were rotated through the various fighter and bomber units in Spain. Although initially equipped with older types such as the He 51 and Ju 52/3M, squadrons were soon testing early examples of the He 111, Bf 109, Do 17 and Ju 87 in combat. Tactics that would later prove so effective in the early stages of World War 2 were also trialled in Spain, with General Wolfram von Richthofen (the Condor Legion's Chief of Staff) developing dive-bombing and close air support tactics and Werner Mölders (the ranking German ace in Spain) devising and perfecting new fighter tactics. Veterans of the war in Spain would return to Germany and pass on their combat experience to the Luftwaffe units in which they served.

The Spanish Civil War also saw the Luftwaffe develop the doctrine and strategy that it would apply to devastating effect during the early stages of World War 2, when it was at its most potent. The Condor Legion developed the new concept of using aircraft for the close support of ground forces (which were often mechanised). Fighter-bombers would attack targets that could not be knocked out with precision by high-level bombers, while dive-bombers performed the role of 'airborne artillery'. The latter had the freedom to operate with relative impunity after escort fighters cleared the skies of aerial opposition. The Condor Legion quickly found that air supremacy was the key to effective Blitzkrieg warfare and when this was not achieved the new German tactics were nowhere near as effective.

It was critical, therefore, that the Luftwaffe's budding fighter pilots received the best possible training prior to being sent to frontline units. As previously noted in this chapter, prior to the official creation of the Luftwaffe, all aerial activity in Germany had been geared towards training because of the ban on military flying under the terms of the 1919 Treaty of Versailles. Those quasi-military aviation organisations that were formed in Germany during the late 1920s and early 1930s functioned under the cover of civilian activities. Although this stalled the development of both combat aircraft and tactics, the focus on flying training provided the newly formed Luftwaffe with plenty of military-trained aircrew. Men came from Deutsche Lufthansa, gliding clubs and, until 1936, the Wehrmacht. However, the latter was expanding rapidly too, and senior officers forbade the Luftwaffe from recruiting from within the Wehrmacht. Conscripts and volunteers would make up the numbers from then on.

In Germany, pilot recruitment and training was strongly influenced by Prussian military tradition. Initially, all future officers and NCOs alike could expect to undertake six months of labour service, organised in a paramilitary fashion, with the Reichsarbeitdienst. Those that were particularly air-minded chose service with the Party-controlled Nationalsozialistisches Fliegerkorps instead, flying gliders. However, with the Luftwaffe desperately short of personnel, labour service was reduced to just three months.

Induction into the Luftwaffe then followed, after which all recruits spent between six and 12 months undertaking basic infantry training at a Flieger-Ersatzabteilung. Once deemed to be an effective infantryman, all recruits were reviewed for possible advancement as pilots. Likely candidates were sent to a Flug-Anwärterkompanie (aircrew candidate company) for evaluation in a series of tests in basic aviation theory.

Most Jagdflieger flying Bf 109Es in 1939-40 would have gone through the full Luftwaffe training course. However, from the autumn of 1940 onwards, with the growing demand for pilots following the commencement of World War 2, training and recruiting staff rationalised and compressed the initial stages of aircrew selection to enable trainees to embark upon the most appropriate training regime more expeditiously. The Flieger-Ersatzabteilung was now replaced by a series of Flieger-Ausbildungsregiments, where recruits would receive basic military training and preliminary aviation instruction. Potential pilots were then sent to undergo the standard selection process within a Flug-Anwärterkompanie, where the rest of their basic training, conducted over a period of three-four months, was completed alongside the aircrew evaluation tests.

Upon assignment to a Flug-Anwärterkompanie, the Flugzeugführer-Anwärter (pilot candidate) would receive instruction in basic flight theory and rudimentary aeronautics in aircraft such as the Bü 131, Ar 66C, He 72 Kaddett, Go 145 and Fw 44 Stieglitz biplane trainers. Assessed for advancement throughout this phase, those candidates displaying the required aptitude were then sent to Flugzeugführerschule A/B as soon as a space became available – typically two months after arriving at the Flug-Anwärterkompanie. Here, flight training proper would be undertaken.

At such schools, students underwent four principal levels of instruction, each requiring qualification for its own license, before advancing to the next stage. These licenses, earned over a period of six to nine months, gave the schools their name. The A1-Schien introduced students to basic practical flying in dual-controlled training aircraft, instructors teaching recruits how to take-off and land, recover from stalls and attain their solo flight rating. Pre-war and through to early 1941, instructors would have been assigned four trainees each – this number rose as the conflict progressed. At the A2-Schien, cadets were required to learn the theory of flight, including aerodynamics, meteorology, flying procedures and aviation law, as well as the practical application of aeronautical engineering, elementary navigation, wireless procedure and Morse code. In the air, they gained more flying experience on larger single-engine two-seat aircraft.

The next level of training, known as the B1-Schien, saw pilots progress onto high-performance single- and twin-engined machines typically fitted with a retractable undercarriage – if destined to fly fighters, older types of combat aircraft such as early Bf 109s would be flown for the first time. Precision landings, night flying and landings and cross-country flying were all tested in this phase of the course. The student pilot would also have to complete at least 50 flights in a B1 category aircraft. Upon graduation from the B1-Schien, students would then undertake training aimed at acquiring the final B2-Schien, having accumulated 100 to 150 hours of flight time over the previous 14 to 17 months.

He 111Ps head for their target during a training sortie in 1939. The crew enjoyed outstanding visibility from the fully glazed nose of the Heinkel bomber, although this also proved to be its weak spot when attacked head-on by Allied fighters.

In late 1940 the Flugzeugführerschule A/B was streamlined to take into account wartime demand for pilots, with a far greater emphasis now being placed on practical flying skills from the outset. The A2 license was dropped, with that phase being amalgamated into the remaining grades.

The A-license generally took three months to complete, with the B phase seeing pilots flying more advanced types. An elementary K1 Kunstflug (stunt-flying) aerobatics course was also included in the latter phase to provide all pilots with a good understanding of rudimentary evasive manoeuvres (barrel rolls, loops and formation splits). This phase also allowed instructors to identify any potential fighter pilots among their students, who thereafter received more flying time than their fellow students.

Upon completion of the B2 phase, the cadet would finally be granted his Luftwaffeflugzeugführerschein (air force pilots' license), accompanied by the highly prized Flugzeugführerabzeichen (pilot's badge) – his 'wings'. After an average of 10-13 months at Flugzeugführerschule A/B, he was now a fully qualified pilot.

It was at this point that new pilots were categorised for service on single- or multi-engined aircraft, with each being assigned to a specialist flying school. Here, he would undergo intensive training for his allotted aircraft type, with potential fighter pilots being sent directly to Jagdfliegervorschulen or Waffenschule for three to four months, where they carried out 50 hours of flying on semi-obsolescent types. For Bf 109E pilots this usually meant Ar 68 and He 51 biplanes, Bf 109B/C/Ds and Ar 96s. By the time he was eventually posted to a frontline unit, a pilot could expect to have 200 hours of flying time under his belt. Officer candidates would have also attended Luftkriegschule to learn tactics, air force law and military discipline, prior to their assignment to a Jagdfliegervorschulen,

The realities of war led the Luftwaffe to further modify the final stages of its training syllabus in 1940, with the creation of Erganzungsgruppen (Operational Training Schools) for the teaching of tactics and further familiarisation with frontline types. In the Jagdwaffe, these units were directly linked to and controlled by operational geschwader. Designated IV Gruppe, the intention of these units was to allow new pilots to gain precious operational experience before being hurled into combat.

All of this meant that when the Luftwaffe engaged the RAF in combat, its crews were already skilled in the art of aerial warfare.

MESSERSCHMITT Bf 109

Designed to meet a 1934 Reichluftfahrtministerium (RLM) requirement for a single-seat monoplane fighter, the original Bf 109 V1 was the winning competitor in a 'fly off' that involved three other designs from proven German aviation companies. Light and small, the first production-standard Bf 109s (B-1 models) to enter service in early 1937 proved their worth during the Spanish Civil War. By the time Germany invaded Poland in September 1939, the re-engined Bf 109E was rolling off the Messerschmitt production line in great quantity, the now-familiar airframe being paired up with the powerful Daimler-Benz DB601. This combination had been tested as long ago as June 1937, when a pre-production aircraft had been flown with a carburetted DB600 fitted in place of the D-model's Junkers Jumo 210Da, but the subsequent availability of the Bf 109E had been hampered by delays in the development of the appreciably more powerful Daimler-Benz engine. However, these problems had been sorted out by early 1939. Built in large numbers and in a great array of sub-variants for the fighter, reconnaissance and fighter-bomber roles, the Bf 109E proved to be the master of all its European contemporaries bar the Spitfire Mk I/II, to which it was considered an equal. Aside from fighting over Poland, the E-model saw combat throughout the Blitzkrieg of 1940 and then in the Battle of Britain that followed.

VALENTINE'S "AIRCRAFT RECOGNITION" CARDS

VALENTINE & SONS, LTD.,
DUNDEE and LONDON.
Printed in Gt. Britain.

JUNKERS Ju 87 STUKA

One of the most feared weapons of the early war years, the Junker Ju 87 struck terror into the hearts of those unfortunate enough to be on the ground beneath it. Dubbed the Stuka (an abbreviation of Stürzkampfflugzeug – dive-bomber aircraft), the prototype had first flown in late 1935 powered by a Rolls-Royce Kestrel engine and with twin fins. By the time it entered series production two years later, the Ju 87B had a solitary fin, a Junkers Jumo 211 engine and large trousered landing gear. It was every inch a dive-bomber, featuring a heavy bomb crutch that swung the weapon clear of the fuselage before it was released. Capable of diving at angles of up to 80 degrees, the aircraft could deliver more than 1,500lb of ordnance with great accuracy. First blooded in Spain by the Condor Legion in 1937, the Ju 87's finest hour came in support of the Blitzkrieg campaign waged by the Wehrmacht in Poland in September 1939 and across western Europe in May-June 1940. Although Ju 87s badly damaged seven airfields and three Chain Home radar stations and destroyed 49 aircraft during the early stages of the Battle of Britain, more often than not formations of Stukas would lose up to half their number or be forced to turn back before reaching their target after coming under sustained attack from Spitfire and Hurricane squadrons. Indeed, during just six days of combat from 12 to 18 August, 41 Ju87s were destroyed. The type was effectively withdrawn from active operations over England in the wake of these losses.

MESSERSCHMITT Bf 110

Designed in 1934-35 to fill the perceived need for a high-speed, long-range, heavily-armed twin-engined fighter, Messerschmitt's Bf 110 Zerstörer (destroyer) fulfilled all these criteria. Seen as the ultimate bomber escort, capable of sweeping the sky clean of enemy fighters, the Bf 110 relied more on its heavy firepower than manoeuvrability to survive in combat. Too late to see action in the Spanish Civil War, the Bf 110C made the aircraft's combat debut over Poland, where it dominated the skies in an environment of overwhelming Luftwaffe air superiority. These successes continued throughout the 'Phoney War' and into the early days of the Blitzkrieg in the west, but come the Battle of Britain, serious flaws in the Zerstörer concept were graphically

exposed. Although the German fighter's forward-firing armament was undeniably lethal, pilots had trouble getting onto the tails of their more agile opponents in order to bring their battery of nose-mounted cannon and machine guns to bear. Furthermore, the solitary 7.9mm machine gun wielded by the radio operator/gunner in the rear cockpit offered the crew little protection against an attack from astern. Lacking speed and acceleration to flee from the RAF fighters, the Bf 110 suffered terrible losses once Fighter Command had got their measure. During August alone, 120 Bf 110s were lost on operations. Ironically, the most effective Zerstörer unit during the campaign was Erprobungsgruppe 210, which was an experimental squadron.

DORNIER Do 17

The least numerous of the trio of medium bombers employed by the Luftwaffe during the Battle of Britain, the Do 17 was derived from a high-speed mailplane/airliner of the early 1930s. Sometimes referred to as the Fliegender Bleistift ('flying pencil'), the aeroplane was converted into a Schnellbomber ('fast bomber') that, in theory at least, would be so fast that it could outrun defending fighters of the period. The Do 17's layout had two engines mounted on a 'shoulder wing' structure, the aircraft also possessing a twin tail fin configuration. Entering frontline service with the Luftwaffe in early 1937, the type soon proved popular among its crews thanks to its exceptional handling qualities, especially at low altitude. This in turn made the Do 17 harder to hit than other German bombers. Indeed, Dornier units specialised in terrain-following raids because the aircraft's robust radial engines performed best at low altitude. In late 1938 Dornier switched production to the definitive Do 17 variant, the Z-model. Driven by the need to provide the bomber with better underside protection and more crew space for maximum operational efficiency, the Do 17Z had an entirely redesigned forward fuselage. Although the most reliable of the Luftwaffe's bombers in the first year of World War 2, the Do 17 lacked the load-carrying capability of the He 111 and the speed of the Ju 88, and production ceased in the early summer of 1940.

"AEROPLANE" PHOTOGRAPH COPYRIGHT

VALENTINE & SONS, LTD., DUNDEE and LONDON. Printed in Gt. Britain.

VALENTINE'S "AIRCRAFT RECOGNITION" CARDS

JUNKERS Ju 88

One of the Luftwaffe's most important and versatile, combat aircraft types, the Ju 88 was developed to answer a requirement for a high-speed medium bomber with a dive-bombing capability. First flown in prototype form in December 1936, production A-1s entered service in September 1939. Boasting a formidable bomb load and good performance, the only down side of the early Ju 88 was its poor defensive armament of just three or four 7.92mm machine guns. The aeroplane was also initially plagued by structural and handling problems, particularly when used as a dive-bomber. These led to the Luftwaffe imposing a series of restrictions on the A-1 in respect to its maximum speed and manoeuvrability. Most of these issues were resolved with the introduction of an interim 'improved Ju 88' in August 1940, designated the A-5. It featured a longer-span, strengthened wing with inset metal-skinned ailerons and a considerably increased bombload. Free of performance restrictions that had hamstrung the A-1, the new aircraft performed admirably in the summer and autumn of 1940 with the handful of gruppen that received it. Thanks to its more modern design and better engines, subsequent versions of the aircraft such as the A-4, which was fitted with twice as many guns, still had sufficient performance available to avoid it being as vulnerable to enemy fighters as the He 111 and Do 17. Continually upgraded and reworked during World War 2, around 2,000 Ju 88 bombers were built per year between 1940-43.

HEINKEL He 111

The Heinkel He 111 was the staple medium bomber of the Luftwaffe's Kampfgeschwader throughout World War 2, some 6,508 examples being built during its nine-year production life. Developed from the He 70 Blitz airliner, which had entered service with Deutsche Lufthansa in 1934, the He 111 retained the former's characteristic elliptical wings and tail surfaces. As with the Blitz, Deutsche Lufthansa also received a small number of airliner-optimised He 111s, designated He 111C/Gs, in 1936. Whilst the transport variant was proving itself over Europe, the bomber version was also being developed by Heinkel. Squadron deliveries began in late 1936, and the following year 30 He 111B-1s saw action during the Spanish Civil War. By the eve of World War 2, the redesigned H- and P-models had begun to enter service, the new variants having the distinctive fully glazed nose area and revised ventral gondola. When Germany invaded Poland on 1 September 1939, the Luftwaffe had 21 gruppen and one staffel equipped with the He 111 – a total of 789 aircraft. The bomber was therefore in the vanguard of operations during this campaign, as well as during the Phoney War in the West, the occupation of Norway in the spring of 1940 and the onslaught on the Low Countries. Indeed, by the time of the Blitzkrieg in the West, Luftflotten 2 and 3 possessed a total of 1,120 twin-engined bombers, of which approximately half were He 111s. Carrying a bigger bombload than any of its contemporaries then in frontline service, the He 111P/H was also heavily utilised during the day and night Blitz on the cities of Britain.

LUFTWAFFE FIGHTER UNIT ORGANISATION

As with the Blitzkrieg in the West, Luftflottenkommando 2 and 3 would be at the forefront of the fighting during the Battle of Britain, controlling all Bf 109 units assigned to the campaign through the offices of Jagdfliegerführer 2 and 3. Unlike British fighter squadrons at the time, which only officially formed into wings as the RAF went on the offensive in 1941, German fighter units had been grouped together pre-war. The Jadgwaffe equivalent to a typical 12-aircraft squadron in Fighter Command in 1940 was the Staffel, which consisted of nine aircraft (rising to as many as 16 as the war progressed). It was led by a Staffelkapitän of oberleutnant or hauptmann rank, who controlled a further 10 pilots and around 80 groundcrew. Staffeln were usually numbered 1, 2, 3 etc.

In 1940, typically, three Staffeln and a Stab (headquarters flight) would be assigned to a single Gruppe, which was the Luftwaffe's basic flying unit for operational and administrative purposes. Normally, one complete Gruppe occupied a single airfield and this was typically the case during the Battle of Britain, with linked Staffeln being spread amongst austere sites in the Pas de Calais, Normandy, Brittany and the Channel Islands. The Gruppenkommandeur was usually a hauptmann or major, and he led somewhere between 35 and 40 pilots and more than 300 groundcrew. Gruppen were usually numbered I., II., III. etc.

The Geschwader was the largest Luftwaffe flying unit to have a fixed strength of aircraft. Eight Jagdgeschwader flew Bf 109Es during the Battle of Britain, with five (JGs 3, 26, 51, 52 and 54) assigned to Luftflottenkommando 2 in Pas de Calais and three to Luftflottenkommando 3 (JGs 2, 27 and 53) in Normandy, Brittany and the Channel Islands. Additionally, Bf 109E fighter-bombers were flown by Erpr.Gr.210's 1 Staffel and II.(Schl.)/LG 2. Assigned some 90-95 aircraft, the Geschwader was usually led by a Kommodore of major, oberstleutnant or oberst rank.

The Jagdgeschwader were in turn locally controlled by Jagdfliegerführer (those involved in the Battle of Britain were numbered 2 and 3), which issued operational directives to the frontline flying units. The Jagdfliegerführer were in turn part of the larger, locally based Fliegerkorps, which were ultimately subordinated to the Luftflottenkommando (of which the Luftwaffe had four in 1940). These were self-contained organisations, each with its own fighter, bomber, reconnaissance, ground attack and transport units.

The Jagdwaffe slowly began to return to the Channel coast in strength during July and early August 1940, some 809 Bf 109Es being in France by 20 July, and this number had increased to 934 by 10 August. Opposing the growing ranks of German fighters were 29 squadrons of Hurricanes (462 aircraft) and 19 squadrons of Spitfires (292 aircraft).

LUFTWAFFE HERALDRY

RAF fighters during the Battle of Britain rarely featured any personal embellishment, with a red or yellow propeller spinner and, very occasionally, a unit marking being the exception to the rule. The Luftwaffe, however, showed little restraint. Only a handful of these markings were officially acknowledged by the Luftwaffe High Command, which had a more relaxed policy when it came to the 'decoration' of frontline aircraft in 1940. Aside from Geschwader badges, aeroplanes were also routinely adorned with Gruppe and Staffel markings, as well as personal insignia.

JG 53

7./JG 54

III./JG 54

8./JG 54

9./JG 54

4.(Schl)/LG 2

III./JG 52

II./JG 51

DEFENDERS of the REALM

Royal Air Force Aircraft and Strength

"The Armourers, accomplishing
the Knights, with busy hammers
closing rivets up, give
Dreadful note of Preparation"

King Henry the Fifth, Act IV, Prologue

William Shakespeare

Defenders of the Realm

At the end of World War 1, Britain had the largest air force ever seen. It was equipped with almost 23,000 aircraft and 293,532 officers, but these numbers had shrunk to just 371 aeroplanes and 31,500 officers by the end of 1919. The first Chief of the Air Staff, Lord Trenchard, successfully fought to keep the Royal Air Force from being disbanded and its aircraft and aircrew absorbed by the Royal Navy and the Army. He also astutely structured the now-tiny RAF as a group of cadres that could be easily expanded when the need arose. Trenchard made sure that training establishments such as the RAF College at Cranwell and the Central Flying School were all created so that recruits joining the air force were given the best possible tuition.

Although all squadrons had a cadre of long-serving permanent commission officers, they were in the main staffed by short service commission personnel. The latter would typically spend only five years in the regular RAF. After this they provided a reserve of trained aircrew who could be refreshed and retrained quickly in a time of crisis. From October 1924, a number of the short service commission aircrew joined the newly formed Auxiliary Air Force after completing their time in the frontline. Here, they served alongside enthusiastic part-timers flying aircraft recently discarded by frontline units.

In the early post-war years, the RAF's primary roles were monitoring and enforcing the armistice in Europe and colonial policing of Britain's burgeoning empire. Home defence was badly neglected in the 1920s, with the RAF fielding a force of just 40 fighters shared between three squadrons. Despite being unable to expand in size, the RAF carefully reorganised from 1925 with the formation of the Air Defence of Great Britain (ADGB). Within it was a 'Fighter Area' that controlled all the fighter aircraft and their airfields. With the threat clearly perceived as coming from the direction of France, a defensive belt of airfields was established from Devizes, in Wiltshire, to Cambridge, curling around London. The belt was devised into eight 15-mile-wide sectors, with one fighter unit per sector, except in the two sectors south and southeast

of London that had two units each. Three more fighter units would be based at coastal airfields and it would be their job to harass enemy formations prior to them reaching the defensive belt. The permanent sector airfields would be augmented by new aerodromes and by satellite and emergency landing grounds.

The foundations for a control and reporting system were also established at this point, ADGB initially relying on the Observer Corps, telephone lines and sound locators – radar and radio would arrive later.

However, it wasn't until 1934 that British military expansion truly got underway when the government voted for a five-year plan for the RAF aimed at increasing its strength by 588 aircraft and 49 squadrons. Two years later the air force was divided into four key commands – Bomber, Fighter, Coastal and Training. In July 1936 Air Marshal Sir Hugh Dowding was appointed Air Officer Commanding-in-Chief of Fighter Command and he would have direct control over the fighter force, anti-aircraft and balloon commands and the Observer Corps.

Shortly after Dowding's appointment he began to implement and refine the defensive belt that had been established a decade earlier – it would soon be dubbed the 'Dowding system'. Fighter Command was divided into four operational groups numbered 10 through 13. No 10 Group covered the southwest, No 11 Group the southeast, No 12 Group started just north of London and continued to North Yorkshire and No 13 Group was responsible for the north of England and all of Scotland and Northern Ireland. The groups were part of a sophisticated defensive system, with each one having its own headquarters that sent out orders to individual sector stations at key airfields. Sectors were given letters for identification purposes, although they were ultimately known by the name of their sector station, which was the airfield controlling them. Defending London and the southeast, No 11 Group would be the vital organisation in the UK's defence in 1940. Its HQ was in Uxbridge and its Sectors (centred on London) were lettered A, B, C, D, E, F and Z, controlled from Tangmere, Kenley, Biggin Hill, Hornchurch, North Weald, Debden and Northolt respectively.

At the heart of this defensive structure was Fighter Command's HQ, Bentley Priory, on the outskirts of London. As Dowding's nerve centre, it boasted a Filter Room to which all information on incoming raids would be sent from radar stations along the coast and Observer Corps posts throughout the country. If the raid was identified as hostile, flight paths of incoming bombers were pinpointed as accurately as possible and this information then passed to the operations room. Here, details of the raid would be displayed on a large plotting table overlaid with a map that showed the various boundaries of the sectors within specific groups. The information would then be passed on to the relevant groups and sector operations rooms, where it was displayed on their situation maps. The great strength of this system was that group commanders had the freedom to decide which of their sectors to alert and sector station commanders were ultimately responsible for the final decision as to which squadrons were to be scrambled to meet the threat.

All the target plotting was eventually done by members of the Women's Auxiliary Air Force. One such plotter was 19-year-old Rosemary Horstmann, who served for three months in the sector operations room at RAF Filton:

'We sat round, or stood round, a large map table of the area in the operations room and with the aid of long sticks, like billiard cues, we pushed little symbols around on this table – showing enemy aircraft coming in and our aircraft going up to intercept them. We were hooked up by headphones to the Observer Corps stations and the Observer Corps people would telephone in to us with information about plots. They would give us a grid reference and we would put a little symbol on to that grid reference and gradually the information would build up.'

The fighters based at the various sector stations and nearby smaller 'satellite' airfields, were the 'teeth' of Fighter Command in 1940, but the pilots flying these aircraft relied on other assets within the command to effectively take the fight to the Luftwaffe. Undoubtedly the most important of these were the chain of radar stations built during the late 1930s along the south and east coasts of England and Scotland. Codenamed Chain Home (CH), the stations (there were 18 between Portsmouth and Aberdeen) were able to detect and track enemy aircraft approaching from medium or high level at distances of more than 100 miles. This equipment proved unable to track aircraft flying at altitudes below 5,000ft however, so in late 1939 the RAF introduced Chain Home Low (CHL) stations that could detect aircraft flying at 2,000ft some 35 miles from the UK coastline.

Radar of this period could not track aircraft overland, so once German aircraft crossed the English coastline, the Observer Corps took over the responsibility of tracking formations. They would pass plot information via landline to their own Group HQ, which in turn relayed details to the Fighter Command Filter Room for onward transmission.

Once airborne, a fighter unit remained under the radio control of one of the sector operations rooms, the fighter controller guiding the squadron until it visually sighted the enemy. At this point the formation leader would call 'Tally Ho!' over the radio, signalling to the controller that he needed no further help from him. Fighter Command squadrons were thoroughly familiar with ground-based fighter control come the summer of 1940, having regularly exercised with this system pre-war.

Although the RAF was in good shape on the ground from a command and control perspective, it would still be up to the young airmen manning Fighter Command's Spitfires, Hurricanes and, to a far lesser extent, Defiants to defend Britain from German invasion. A large number of pilots would be needed to fly these aircraft in the frontline, and it was obvious that the existing Flying Training Schools (for short service officers and airmen pilots) and RAF College training (for permanent officers) output of around 400 pilots a year was grossly inadequate for the task.

Back in 1933, the RAF had already taken steps to improve the volume of its pilot training by establishing a handful of civilian-manned Elementary and Reserve Flying Training Schools (E&RFTSs), equipped with Gipsy Moths, Tiger Moths and Blackburn B2s. That same year it had also established a standardised training programme for future officer pilots at RAF College Cranwell. When Training Command was established in 1936, the Air Ministry also created the RAF Volunteer Reserve (RAFVR) to train 800 pilots a year. Open to all comers, no matter what their financial or social status, this scheme proved so popular that by 1940 a third of Fighter Command's pilots had joined as RAFVRs – a considerable number served with frontline units as sergeant pilots. Prior to this, all recruits entered either as permanent or short service commission officers and NCOs, or via the Auxiliary Air Force.

Amongst the pilots to experience the RAF's revised pilot training set up was future Spitfire I ace Al Deere, who was one of 12 New Zealanders selected to travel to the UK in September 1937 – many young men from across the Empire took up short service commissions in the air force during this period. Deere was initially sent to the de Havilland Civil School of Flying, where he underwent an ab initio flying course for the next three months prior to being accepted into the RAF. Pilots were then asked to make a choice as to whether they wanted to fly bombers or fighters – Deere, of course, chose the latter.

Sir Robert Alexander Watson-Watt, widely regarded as the 'founding father' of radar.

During the Battle of Britain the Observer Corps was at full stretch, operating 24 hours a day, seven days a week, plotting enemy aircraft and passing this essential information to Fighter Command Groups and Sector Controls.

A simplified graphic representation of Fighter Command's outstanding operations control system, which was used to stunning effect during the Battle of Britain.

An example of a Chain Home Low station, this one being situated at Hopton-on-Sea.

Duxford's operations block, which houses the airfield's original Operations Room.

INTRICATE AND FLEXIBLE: THE OPERATIONS CONTROL

A WAAF radar operator plots aircraft on the cathode ray tube in the receiver room of a Chain Home station.

When war was clearly imminent, a permanent underground operations room was constructed at Bentley Priory. It duplicated the same layout as the original room, but 40ft below ground. WAAFs in the Operations Room received information of incoming raids via their headsets and used billiard-style cues to move the unit symbols on the situation-map table and update the picture for the commanders seated around the balcony above.

Following graduation from the E&RFTS, pilots destined to be commissioned then spent two weeks undergoing officer training at RAF Uxbridge, prior to heading to a Flying Training School. Deere went to No 6 FTS at Netheravon in Wiltshire, where he flew Harts. Upon completion of this phase of his training, he was awarded his pilot's Wings, after which he flew Fury fighters. Completing his nine months of flying training in August 1938, Deere was duly posted to Hornchurch, in No 11 Group, to fly Gladiators with No 54 Squadron.

Like most pre-war fighter pilots already serving with frontline or auxiliary units, Al Deere made the transition from biplane to monoplane at squadron level, as there were insufficient Spitfires and Hurricanes available to supply them to Training Command. Most pilots had plenty of flying experience under their belts by the time the switch was made, and the change in types posed few problems, as Deere noted:

'On 6 March 1939, I flew my first Spitfire. The transition from slow biplanes to the faster monoplanes was effected without fuss, and in a matter of weeks we were nearly as competent on Spitfires as we had been on Gladiators. Training on Spitfires followed the same pattern as on Gladiators, except that we did a little more cine-gun work to get practice on the new reflector gunsight with which the aircraft was fitted.'

Fighter Command also established several Group Pools in 1939 and equipped them with a handful of Hurricanes and Spitfires. New pilots would thus be able to get a precious few flying hours in their logbooks on-type before joining Fighter Command proper.

With the declaration of war, all E&RFTSs were brought within the RAF Training Command structure as Elementary Flying Training Schools. Once finished here, pupils would then progress to Service Flying Training Schools (boosted in number from six to 11 by early 1940). The types operated at both stages in the training process remained much the same during the first 18 months of the war, although the interwar biplane fighters seen at the SFTSs slowly began to be replaced by more Harvards and the all-new Miles Master.

The Group Pool system, from which operational squadrons were able to draw replacement pilots and thus relinquish their own training responsibilities so as to concentrate on performing combat missions, soon showed signs of failure in wartime. Indeed, literally thousands of trainee pilots (many with considerable flying hours already in their logbooks) were transferred into other trades in late 1939 and early 1940 because of a chronic shortage of monoplane fighter types

within the Group Pools. Spitfires and Hurricanes were urgently needed in the frontline, leaving none for training purposes. In the spring of 1940, all Group Pools were re-designated Operational Training Units (OTUs) within Training Command. The OTUs eventually succeeded where the Group Pools had failed, thanks to an influx of often combat-weary fighters and equally battle-seasoned pilots to instruct would-be frontline aviators.

When losses began to mount in August 1940, OTU courses for new pilots were drastically cut in length from several months to just four weeks. As a result of this, Fighter Command began receiving replacement pilots who had not yet mastered the Spitfire or Hurricane, and who had received little more than basic training in night flying, navigation or gunnery – indeed, a number of pilots had never fired their guns, period, prior to engaging the enemy for the first time.

Despite cutting corners in pilot training, still more were needed as replacements as the Luftwaffe continued to exact a heavy toll on the RAF. With no time to train them from scratch, Fighter Command sought out pilots from other commands within the RAF, as well as the Fleet Air Arm. The best pilots from Army Co-operation, Coastal and Bomber Commands were also posted in, as were 75 partly trained naval pilots. Combat-seasoned fighter pilots also came from Poland, Czechoslovakia, Belgium and France, having fled to Britain following the German occupation of their respective countries.

These were the men that manned the Spitfire, Hurricane and Defiant squadrons that helped defend Britain in the summer of 1940.

VICKERS-SUPERMARINE SPITFIRE

The only British fighter to remain in production throughout World War 2, the exploits of the Supermarine Spitfire are legendary. More than 20,000 were produced in mark numbers ranging from I through to 24, this total also including over 1,000 built as dedicated Seafire fleet fighters for the Royal Navy. Designed by Reginald J. Mitchell following his experiences with the RAF's Schneider Trophy-winning Supermarine floatplanes of the 1920s and 30s, prototype Spitfire K5054 first took to the skies on 5 March 1936, powered by the soon to be equally famous Rolls-Royce Merlin I engine. However, due to production problems encountered with the revolutionary stressed-skin construction of the fighter, it was to be another two-and-a-half years before the first examples entered service with Fighter Command. Spitfire Mk Is and IIs served only briefly in frontline squadrons with the RAF (exclusively on the Channel Front) once the war had started, but their pilots were responsible for achieving impressive scores against the all-conquering Luftwaffe in 1940. In the Battle of Britain a total of 529 German aircraft were shot down by Spitfires serving with 20 units of Fighter Command. Conversely, 361 Spitfires were lost and 352 damaged during this period. Finally, of the 10 top-scoring squadrons in Fighter Command, six of them were equipped with Spitfires. Although the early mark Spitfires were notorious for their light armament, overheating engines due to inadequate cooling and short range, many of the pilots that flew Mk Is and IIs regarded these first production machines as the best handling of the breed due to their excellent power-to-weight ratio and beautifully harmonised flying controls.

SPITFIRE

GLOSTER GLADIATOR

The ultimate (and final) British biplane fighter of them all, the Gladiator started life as a company private venture, based very much on its predecessor, the Gauntlet. Although equipped with four guns, the design still embraced the 'old' technology of doped fabric over its wood and metal ribbed and stringered fuselage and wings. Following its first flight in September 1934, the Gladiator I was swiftly put into production, with Gloster eventually building 231 examples. It made its service debut in January 1937 and went on to fly with 26 RAF fighter squadrons. The Mk II soon followed, the main differences being a slightly more powerful Mercury engine driving a Fairey fixed-pitch three-bladed metal propeller. The replacement of the Gladiator

by the Hurricane and Spitfire in Fighter Command was underway when war was declared. By the time of the Battle of Britain, only a handful of Gladiators remained in frontline service with the Shetland Fighter Flight defending Scapa Flow. An expanded flight equipped with Gladiators was also established at Roborough – a small grass airstrip unsuitable for monoplane fighters – to protect Plymouth's naval dockyard. The Shetland Gladiators eventually moved south to St Eval, in Cornwall, and became No 247 Squadron on 1 August. The unit failed to engage the enemy during the Battle of Britain despite numerous raids being made on Plymouth, the Gladiator lacking the speed to intercept high-flying bombers.

BOULTON PAUL "DEFIANT" 2 Seater Fighter.

BOULTON PAUL DEFIANT

The final result of the turret fighter concept evolved by the RAF in the early 1930s, the Defiant enjoyed a less than successful career as a frontline fighter in the dangerous skies over southern England during the summer of 1940. Built to combine the strengths of new monoplane fighter design with the latest in turret weaponry, the Defiant struggled against single-seat opposition both in terms of speed and agility due to the weight of its two-man crew and its primary armament. Entering service with No 264 Squadron in December 1939, the Defiant initially proved to be very successful in its designated role of bomber destroyer. The aeroplane was less effective against enemy fighters, except when it was mistaken for a Spitfire or Hurricane in the heat of battle and

attacked from above and behind. Otherwise, the Defiant proved to be an easy target for the Bf 109E, with 14 having been lost by the end of Dunkirk. No 264 Squadron had, rather optimistically, claimed 65 aircraft destroyed in return – 37 of them in one day! By the summer of 1940, No 141 Squadron had also been formed with the Defiant. Flying from West Malling, it served with No 11 Group from 3 June until 21 July, when it was withdrawn after suffering heavy losses to Bf 109s in its first action. Having made good its 'Dynamo' losses, No 264 Squadron only lasted six days in the frontline during the Battle of Britain, during which time it had 11 aircraft destroyed and five pilots and nine air gunners killed.

HAWKER HURRICANE

The arrival of the Hurricane in the frontline in December 1937 saw the RAF finally make the jump from biplane to monoplane fighters. The aircraft owed much to Hawker's ultimate biplane design, the Fury, both types being built around an internal 'skeleton' of four wire-braced alloy and steel tube longerons — this structure was renowned for both its simplicity of construction and durability. The Hurricane also benefitted from Hawker's long-standing partnership with Rolls-Royce, whose newly developed Merlin I engine proved to be the ideal powerplant. Toting eight 0.303in machine guns and capable of speeds in excess of 300mph, the Hurricane I was the world's most advanced fighter when issued to the RAF. Although technically eclipsed by the Spitfire come the summer of 1940, Hurricanes nevertheless outnumbered the former type during the Battle of Britain by three-to-one and actually downed more Luftwaffe aircraft than the Vickers-Supermarine fighter. Indeed, it is estimated that Hurricane pilots were responsible for four-fifths of all enemy aircraft destroyed in the period July to October 1940, with squadrons claiming 1,593 victories. This averaged out to 44.25 kills per unit, compared with more than 60 for squadrons equipped with Spitfires. Having taken over-claiming into account, the leading Hurricane unit with substantiated kills was No 303 'Polish' Squadron, with 51.5 victories (it claimed 121), followed by No 501 Squadron with 40.25 victories (it claimed 101). The latter unit also holds the record for the highest number of days engaged (35) of any Fighter Command squadron during the Battle of Britain. Conversely, No 501 Squadron also suffered more losses than any of its contemporaries, having an astonishing 41 Hurricanes destroyed.

HURRICANE

BRISTOL BLENHEIM

Bristol's venerable Blenheim was the result of a speculative private venture on the part of the manufacturers. Unencumbered by restrictions on the aircraft's weight, powerplants, general layout or radius of action, the Bristol design team produced a sleek twin-engined machine known as the Type 142. First flown at Filton on 12 April 1935, the aircraft's performance sent ripples of concern through the RAF when it was discovered that its top speed was 30mph faster than Fighter Command's then new biplane fighter, the Gloster Gauntlet I. Christened the Blenheim, the Air Ministry ordered 150 airframes and the first of these entered service with the RAF in March 1937. With war clouds looming at the time of the Munich Crisis of September 1938, the replacement of the biplane Demon with more modern equipment became urgent. A Blenheim I was duly fitted with a trial installation of an under-fuselage gun pack containing four Browning machine guns. Following the trials, the first of almost 150 surplus Blenheim Is (most UK-based Blenheim bomber squadrons had replaced their Mk Is with the improved Mk IV) were modified for the long-range fighter. Thus equipped, the aircraft were re-designated Blenheim IFs. The first of these new 'fighters' were delivered to No 25 Squadron at Hawkinge and No 23 Squadron at Wittering in December 1938. By the summer of 1940, Fighter Command Blenheim IFs were tasked with performing nightfighter duties, while Coastal Command's trio of Blenheim IVF units (Nos 235, 236 and 248 Squadrons) also saw considerable action in their longer-range aircraft, crews bravely flying local defence patrols when incoming air raids were detected.

RAF HERALDRY
CIGARETTE CARDS

Published by John Player & Sons Cigarettes in 1937, a 50-strong set of cards illustrated the official squadron badges of fighter, bomber, army co-operation, torpedo-bomber, general reconnaissance and bomber transport units of the rapidly expanding RAF. Thanks to the annual Hendon air pageant, the introduction of new fighters and bombers like the Hurricane, Spitfire and Blenheim and their growing presence in the skies of southern England, the British general public were rapidly becoming more air-minded. Hence the commissioning of this series of cards. John Player & Sons was one of the first British tobacco companies to include sets of general interest cards in its cigarette packs, starting in the early 1890s. More than 200 sets were produced overall.

No. 1 (FIGHTER) SQUADRON, R.A.F.

No. 17 (FIGHTER) SQUADRON, R.A.F.

No. 19 (FIGHTER) SQUADRON, R.A.F.

No. 54 (FIGHTER) SQUADRON, R.A.F.

No. 56 (FIGHTER) SQUADRON, R.A.F.

No. 64 (FIGHTER) SQUADRON, R.A.F.

No. 23 (FIGHTER) SQUADRON,
R.A.F.

No. 32 (FIGHTER) SQUADRON,
R.A.F.

No. 41 (FIGHTER) SQUADRON,
R.A.F.

No. 43 (FIGHTER) SQUADRON,
R.A.F.

No. 66 (FIGHTER) SQUADRON,
R.A.F.

No. 74 (FIGHTER) SQUADRON,
R.A.F.

No. 111 (FIGHTER) SQUADRON,
R.A.F.

No. 151 (FIGHTER) SQUADRON,
R.A.F.

The COMMANDERS

Royal Air Force versus Luftwaffe

....

"Be not Afraid of Greatness:
Some are Born great
some Achieve Greatness
and some have
Greatness Thrust upon them"

Twelfth Night, Act II, Scene V

William Shakespeare

AIR CHIEF MARSHAL
SIR HUGH DOWDING

V

REICHSMARSCHALL
HERMANN GÖRING

The Commanders

AIR CHIEF MARSHAL
SIR HUGH DOWDING

ACM Sir Hugh Dowding, Commander-in-Chief (C-in-C) of Fighter Command, was described by Gen Sir Frederick Pile, C-in-C Anti-Aircraft Command, as 'a difficult man, a self-opinionated man, a most determined man and a man who knew more than anybody about all the aspects of aerial warfare'.

It is, therefore, astonishing that throughout June 1940, Dowding was under notice from the Air Ministry to retire. Having antagonised Churchill in mid-May when he pleaded the case for not sending more Hurricanes to France, the eccentric Dowding was very much a loner with few friends in high places.

Born in 1882, Dowding experienced a conventional, dutiful Victorian middle-class upbringing. Following his father to Winchester public school, he subsequently entered the Royal Military Academy. Becoming a gunner, Dowding served in a succession of British Army garrisons around the world. Showing an interest in aviation, he learned to fly at Brooklands and when war was declared with Germany in August 1914, Dowding was transferred to the RFC.

With the formation of the new RAF on 1 April 1918, Dowding became a career officer and was appointed C-in-C Fighter Command upon its formation in 1936. He duly set about providing the British Isles with a proper, co-ordinated, fighter defence for the first time. Dowding was well suited to this task, as he had an instinctive understanding of the essentials of air warfare. Once the Battle of Britain started, Dowding's strategy of carefully managing his resources paid dividends. He made sure that he kept sufficient reserves ready to reinforce the frontline as its individual squadrons became exhausted. Fully aware that he was fighting a battle of attrition with the Luftwaffe, Dowding never lost sight of the need to be able to fight again tomorrow, and next week if need be. His reward for employing the right strategy during the Battle of Britain was dismissal on 17 November 1940, having been bluntly told that 'The Air Council have no further work to offer you'.

RAF Fighter Command Headquarters at Bentley Priory, Stanmore, Middlesex.

The complete antithesis of Dowding, as Air Minister and Commander-in-Chief of the Luftwaffe, Hermann Göring was the man Hitler looked to when it came to gaining control of the skies over Britain. One of the Führer's closest advisors and his designated successor, Göring was also the most powerful military leader in Germany in 1940.

Born in 1893, he was the son of a retired government official. In the lead up to World War 1, Göring became an infantry officer and saw extensive service in the trenches before he was hospitalised. Unable to return to the fighting as a soldier, he was eventually accepted as an aviator and survived the war with 22 victories to his credit. Göring also received the coveted Pour le Mérite.

War hero Göring was a powerful asset to the National Socialist Party when he joined in 1922. In his early years he ran its 'Brownshirts' paramilitary wing. He was shot in the groin during the ill-fated Munich Putsch in November 1923 and was spirited away to Austria to recuperate. Having recovered from morphine addiction, in 1927 Göring returned to Germany and as the Nazi Party rose to power he became President of the Reichstag and then Prime Minister of Prussia. He also organised the stormtroopers, formed the Gestapo and set up the first concentration camps.

Exploiting his position of power, Göring enjoyed a lifestyle more suited to a medieval lord than a political heavyweight and military commander. Grand estates, hunting lodges and art collections all became his as he accepted bribes and confiscated Jewish property. Hitler tolerated Göring's excesses, however, because he was a consummate politician, a skilful schemer and was totally committed to the Nazi cause.

Despite his command of what was the world's greatest air force in the summer of 1940, Göring had made no attempt to understand the nature and limitations of air power in the lead up to the Battle of Britain. Although possessing a formidable intellect, he was not a 'military thinker'. Indeed, Göring took no interest in technology and saw aerial combat merely in terms of shooting down as many of the enemy's aeroplanes as possible. Ultimately, Göring's concept of command, and his bombastic approach to winning the Battle of Britain, sealed the Luftwaffe's fate.

AIR VICE-MARSHAL
KEITH PARK

In charge of No 11 Group, New Zealander Keith Park was handpicked for this critically important position by Hugh Dowding due to his vast experience of all aspects of fighter direction. Indeed, as Dowding's Senior Air Staff Officer (SASO), Park had done more than most to help prepare Fighter Command for war. Familiar with the way his superior thought and operated, Park was the ideal choice as Air Officer Commanding (AOC) in No 11 Group – a role he assumed in April 1940. Born of Scottish parents in 1892, Park volunteered for service in World War 1 and survived the debacle at Gallipoli in April 1915. Posted to the Somme as an artillery officer the following year, he was seriously wounded by a shell blast and declared unfit for active duty. Park then joined the RFC and he eventually became an ace flying Bristol F2 Fighters with No 48 Squadron. A squadron commander by war's end, Park remained in the newly created RAF. When made AOC No 11 Group, Park was quick to devise tactics for his fighters that played up to their strengths and made the most of the intricate defence system he had helped Dowding create. Arguably the RAF's greatest tactical air commander, Park, like Dowding, was posted out of Fighter Command shortly after the conclusion of the Battle of Britain.

AIR VICE-MARSHAL
TRAFFORD LEIGH-MALLORY

Irked that he had been left in charge of No 12 Group since 1937, rather than being promoted to command the vital No 11 Group, Trafford Leigh-Mallory became one of Dowding's toughest critics during 1940. Like Park, he had served with distinction in the RFC during World War 1. Indeed, he had pioneered the use of aircraft against tanks on the Western Front. Gaining a reputation as an intellectual and strategic thinker, Leigh-Mallory had a personal disliking of Keith Park who had been promoted over him. During the Battle of Britain Leigh-Mallory expended more effort in winning a prominent role for No 12 Group and its squadrons than supporting Park's direct requests for assistance. Leigh-Mallory claimed that his 'Big Wing' massed fighter formation, devised with the assistance of the charismatic Sqn Ldr Douglas Bader, was being prevented from operating successfully by the tactics of Park and Dowding. Park countered these claims by stating that there was not the time to form up such 'Big Wings' before the German bombers had hit their targets – his airfields in No 11 Group. Throughout the Battle of Britain Leigh-Mallory worked energetically in political circles to bring about the removal of Park from command of No 11 Group. He achieved his goal in November 1940.

AIR VICE-MARSHAL
SIR QUINTIN BRAND

South African-born Quintin Brand took over the newly formed No 10 Group in July 1940, just weeks after it had been established to allow neighbouring No 11 Group to function more efficiently by taking over responsibility for the defence of southwest England and South Wales. Reflecting the lesser importance of this area, Brand's group was initially given just seven single-engined fighter squadrons. Unlike Leigh-Mallory in No 12 Group, Brand actively supported Keith Park in the use of small, rapidly deployed, groups of fighters to intercept Luftwaffe formations during the Battle of Britain. He also provided material support to No 11 Group whenever it was required. Like Park, Brand had become an ace flying fighters in the RFC during World War 1 – one of his victories was over a Gotha bomber that had attacked London at night. He was knighted in 1920 for a long-distance flight he participated in from London to Cape Town and subsequently served in a number of senior posts within the RAF both at home and abroad, prior to taking charge of No 10 Group. Brand also paid the price for being an ally of Dowding and Park, being side-lined in Training Command after the Battle of Britain.

GENERALFELDMARSCHALL
ALBERT KESSELRING

GENERALFELDMARSCHALL
HUGO SPERRLE

GENERALOBERST
HANS-JÜRGEN STUMPFF

Commander of Luftlotte 2, Albert Kesselring was a career army officer who had served during World War 1. Having reluctantly accepted a transfer to the then still top secret Luftwaffe in 1933 to help with its development, he learned to fly at the age of 48 when appointed as its Head of Administration. Made Göring's Chief of Staff three years later, Kesselring became head of Luftflotte 1 shortly before the start of World War 2. After overseeing a successful campaign in Poland, Kesselring was appointed head of Luftflotte 2 to spearhead the Blitzkrieg in the West. He remained in this position throughout the Battle of Britain, with Luftflotte 2 initially being responsible for the bombing of south-eastern England and the London area from its bases in Belgium, Holland and northern France. As the battle progressed, however, command responsibility shifted, with Generalfeldmarschall Hugo Sperrle's Luftflotte 3 taking more responsibility for night Blitz attacks while the main daylight operations fell to Luftflotte 2.

The most experienced air force officer in Germany when the Luftwaffe was revealed to the world in 1935, Hugo Sperrle had originally joined the Germany army as early as 1903. He transferred to the Luftstreitkräfte (German Army Air Service) shortly after the outbreak of World War 1, as an observer. Serving in the Freikorps and then the Reichswehr in logistics and army command positions during the 1920s and early 1930s, Sperrle joined the Luftwaffe in 1935. The following year he became the first commander of the Condor Legion in Spain, and by September 1939 Sperrle was in charge of Luftflotte 3. Although his air fleet saw no action in Poland, it was committed to combat in France from May, providing support for the Wehrmacht through tactical bombing. Luftflotte 3 subsequently played a major role in the Battle of Britain, its units flying from bases in northern France. In September 1940 Sperrle was involved in a heated debate with Hermann Göring after the latter changed strategies and switched to bombing British cities rather than RAF airfields.

Hans-Jürgen Stumpff commanded the Luftwaffe's third air fleet, Luftflotte 5, during the Battle of Britain, its aircraft carrying out raids on targets in Scotland and northern England from airfields in Scandinavia. Yet another veteran of service in the German army during World War 1, Stumpff served as a staff officer in the Reichswehrministerium during the Weimar Republic in the 1920s. In September 1933 he became head of personnel in the then clandestine Luftwaffe, before serving as its Chief of Staff from June 1937 to January 1939. Stumpff assumed command of Luftflotte 5 from Generalfeldmarschall Erhard Milch in May 1940, the air fleet having been formed the previous month for the invasion of Norway. The smallest of the Luftwaffe's Luftflotten, its Bf 109s lacked the range to escort the He 111s and Ju 88s sent to attack targets in Britain on 15 August 1940. The Bf 110s that were despatched as escorts instead proved to be as vulnerable as the medium bombers, resulting in Luftflotte 5 suffering heavy losses to RAF fighters. Stumpff's units played no significant part in the Battle of Britain after this debacle, with many of their aircraft and aircrew being sent south to reinforce Luftflotten 2 and 3.

PHASE ONE

The Channel Front

··

"Once More unto
the Breach dear friends
Once More"

King Henry the Fifth, Act III, Scene I

William Shakespeare

The Channel Front

The Battle of Britain has been split into four distinct phases by historians, with the official start of the campaign being recognised as 10 July 1940. Air Chief Marshal Dowding later noted in his report to the Secretary of State for Air, that this was the day the Germans employed 'the first really big formations – 70 aircraft – intended primarily to bring our fighter defences to battle on a large scale'. However, for the Fighter Command pilots who had tangled with the Luftwaffe over France, Belgium and Holland since the evacuation of Dunkirk, the battle had commenced in earnest weeks before.

Since late June, the Luftwaffe had been mining the approaches to British ports and sending out Bf 109Es (primarily from JG 26 and JG 53, as the remaining Jagdgeschwader were still making good losses from the Battle of France) on deadly 'freie jagd' sweeps over southern England in search of No 11 Group fighters. The effectiveness of the latter was graphically proven by the loss of 28 RAF fighters and 18 pilots in the 10 days prior to the 'opening' of the Battle of Britain. Once again operating without the benefits of their highly effective defence system and saddled with all the disadvantages that had characterised their operations over Dunkirk, the Spitfire and Hurricane pilots charged with flying offensive patrols over the French side of the Channel viewed these missions with dissatisfaction. One such individual was No 32 Squadron's Flt Lt Pete Brothers, flying from Biggin Hill:

'After Dunkirk we were doing these utterly stupid offensive patrols in wing strength at around 15,000ft so as to demonstrate air superiority. We would be detailed to fly down the French coast, cross in at Calais and then fly down to Amiens, before turning around and coming back up the coast. The snag was that the Germans [based at nearby Abbeville and Merville] took no notice of you on the way in. They would just watch you fly past, waiting until you were on your way home, when they knew you were getting short on fuel. By then you were heading north, with the sun behind you, which was just what they wanted. They could take off and climb up and attack you from behind when you were on the way home. This happened time and time again, and we were getting hammered for no reason.

'We decided that these sweeps were a terrible waste of time because all we did was suffer casualties without achieving very much success. And finally, fortunately, "Stuffy" Dowding himself came down to Hawkinge, where we were sitting on the grass awaiting the order to scramble. By then I was getting rather tired, and I duly told him what I thought about these bloody silly patrols. He grunted and said nothing. We flew one the next day and they were stopped.'

The Luftwaffe was also suffering losses during this period, especially amongst the reconnaissance aircraft that were being sent over southeast England to photograph targets for the Kanalkampf (Channel Battle) offensive that would see British convoys and coastal targets attacked in an increasingly powerful succession of raids. Although the Bf 109 pilots flying 'freie jagd' sweeps were still enjoying the upper hand against Fighter Command, those charged with escorting the slower bomber and reconnaissance aircraft were beginning to realise that such missions were fraught with danger – a precursor of things to come for the Jagdwaffe. An early casualty during just such a sortie was Leutnant Albert Striberny of 3./LG 2, who was in fact the last German pilot to be shot down before the Battle of Britain officially commenced:

'Having reached an altitude of 4,500m over the Channel, we found ourselves in sunshine, but saw that there were a lot of cumulus clouds over the English coast and Dover. The [photo-reconnaissance] Do 17, contrary to our agreement, dived into the clouds, and the three of us Bf 109s had to move together and follow him. At about 1,700m the clouds ended and together we flew over Dover. Besides photographing, the Do 17 threw out some small bombs and then climbed back into cloud, and we again joined up and followed. When the clouds ended, I quickly noticed the Do 17 near us, but then, much higher, saw the sun shining on many aircraft – Spitfires!

'Our situation was bad – low speed due to climbing through the cloud and so many aircraft coming down on us with the advantage of speed. I think now of the clear silhouette of our three aircraft against the white clouds.

'In spite of our efforts to try and gain more speed, in no time they were on us and the battle was short. While I was behind a Spitfire, another was behind me [Flt Lt Basil Way of No 54 Squadron]. I heard the sound as if one throws peas against a metal sheet and my cockpit was full of dark smoke. I felt splashes of fuel on my face, so I switched off the electrical system, dived back into the cloud and threw off the canopy. The smoke disappeared and I could breathe freely. I also noticed that white streams of glycol were trailing from the wings. Whilst diving, I tried several times to start the engine, switching on the electrical system, but in vain. When I came out of cloud I decided to bale out and undid the clasp of my seat belt and was about to climb onto the seat and jump when I thought of the high speed of the aircraft and I was afraid of being thrown against the tailplane, so I pulled back on the stick and slowed the aircraft down. This took a matter of seconds. I did a half roll and fell out.'

Oberst Johannes Fink, Geschwaderkommodore of KG 2, was appointed Kanalkampfführer and he was tasked with clearing the Straits of Dover of British aircraft and shipping. He was to use his three Gruppen of Do 17s, together with two Gruppen of Ju 87s, the Bf 110s of ZG 26 and the Bf 109s of JGs 26 and 53 to achieve this – a tiny force for such a daunting task. Bombers were duly sent out with substantial fighter escorts, these missions having the dual aim of sinking British vessels and knocking out coastal targets and also exhausting Fighter Command. In the vanguard of the attacks on 10 July was the Gruppenkommandeur of III./KG 2, Major Werner Kreipe:

'The convoy [codenamed "Bread"] had been sighted between Dover and Dungeness. Our briefing took only a few minutes, and within half-an-hour of being airborne we had sighted the coast of Kent. The Channel was bathed in brilliant sunshine. A light haze hung over the English coast and there, far below us, was the convoy, like so many toy ships with wispy wakes fanning out behind. As soon as we were observed, the ships of the convoy dispersed, the merchantmen manoeuvring violently and the escorting warships moving out at full speed. Anti-aircraft shells peppered the sky. Our fighters now appeared. We made our first bomb run and fountains leapt up around the ships. By now the fighter squadrons of the RAF had joined in, and the sky was a twisting, turning melee of fighters.

'My wing was in the air for three hours in all. We reported one heavy cruiser and four merchant ships sunk, one merchant ship damaged and 11 British fighters shot down or damaged. We had lost two bombers, two twin-engined fighters and three single-engined fighters during the course of this engagement.'

The claims for vessels sunk were, in reality, wide of the mark, as only a single small ship was lost. The RAF had managed to down 16 German aircraft for the loss of six fighters. In order to achieve these

successes, however, Fighter Command had had to fly an astonishing 600 sorties. This hectic pace would be sustained throughout the Kanalkampf, allowing the RAF to retain a convincing kill-loss ratio. Most of the aircraft brought down would be bombers, which were effectively acting as bait for the Jagdwaffe formations flying above the Do 17s, He 111s, Ju 87s and Ju 88s, waiting to swoop down and pick off the Fighter Command aeroplanes. For the most part, the RAF pilots killed during this early phase were veterans of the Battle of France and the Dunkirk operation, and they would be impossible to replace at short notice.

Although No 11 Group bore the brunt of the action during Kanalkampf, No 10 Group became involved when the Luftwaffe targeted the naval base at Portland and convoys off the southwest coast. One such mission occurred on 18 July, when Ju 88s from I./ and II./KG 54 went after a convoy southeast of Swanage. Spitfires from No 609 Squadron were scrambled from Warmwell in response as Flt Lt Frank Howell explained in a letter he wrote to his parents shortly thereafter:

'Bags of excitement here – almost too much. The other day, Red Section was sent up to 18,000ft over Portland. It was a mucky day, and we had to go up through two layers of cloud. Bandy Control gave us a bearing to fly on and said that we ought to meet a Jerry, possibly two, which were in the vicinity. He had hardly finished speaking when out of the cloud loomed a Ju 88. Whoopee! I told my Nos 2 and 3 to look out for enemy fighters while I made an almost head-on attack at it. I don't think he liked that one little bit because he turned over and went split arse for the sea, releasing four large bombs, and doing over 350mph. I got in another attack and got his port motor. I was going to do a third when I saw the other chaps screaming down at him. So I let them have a go, being a generous chap!

'Just then I smelt a nasty smell! An 'orrid smell! I looked at the dials and things and saw that the coolant temperature was right off the clock, about 180°C, and the oil temperature was at 95°C and going up. The bugger had shot me in the radiator! White fumes began pouring back into the cockpit, so I thought that was not really good enough. The poor old motor began to seize up. I called up Bandy and said, "Hello Bandy Control, Red One calling – I am going to bale out four miles off Poole!" The silly controller at the other end, of course, couldn't hear me and asked me to repeat. Bah. Still, I still had 5000ft, so I told him

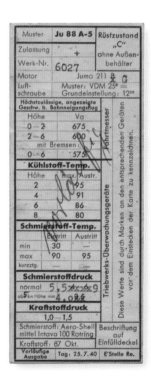

Records show that this German reconnaissance photograph of Dover harbour was taken at 14.26hrs on 7 August 1940 from 3,500m.

again and wished him a very good afternoon, and stepped smartly from the aircraft.

'I read something about pulling a ripcord so had a grope, found same, pulled same and sat up with a jerk, but with no damage to the important parts. Everything was lovely – quiet as a church, a lovely day, a spot of sun, three ships two miles away who would be bound to see me! Found myself still holding the ripcord handle, so I flung it away – chucked my helmet away too, but kept the goggles! Undid my shoes, blew up my Mae West and leaned back and admired the scenery. The water quite suddenly came very close – a swish and then I began my final swim for the season. I set out with a lusty crawl for Bournemouth, thinking I might shoot a hell of a line staggering up the beach with beauteous barmaids dashing down the beach with bottles of brandy. Instead, the current was taking me out to sea, and I was unceremoniously hauled on board a 12ft motorboat. Still, the navy pushed out the boat, and the half tumbler of whisky went down with a rush.'

The much-vaunted Stukas had been committed to the convoy offensive from the very start and although they carried out some highly accurate attacks on the British vessels in the Channel, they also proved to be terribly vulnerable to defending RAF fighters. II./StG 1 was on the receiving end of a mauling on 20 July when it attacked Convoy Bosom as it sailed east past Dover. The Ju 87s had been provided with an escort of 50+ Bf 109s and Bf 110s, which were engaged by 28 Spitfires and Hurricanes. Flying one of the latter aircraft was Flt Lt Pete Brothers:

'It was a Saturday, and following what was becoming normal practice, we deployed to Hawkinge from Biggin Hill, where we spent a quiet morning and what turned into a noisy afternoon.

'At about 17.00hrs No 32 Squadron was ordered to patrol over Convoy Bosom, which was some 10 miles east of Dover, steaming northeastwards. Led by Sqn Ldr John "The Baron" Worrall, the nine of us, happy to be relieved of the boredom of waiting around on the ground, took off to perform the dull job patrolling up and down a line of ships, which we duly did for a while. Over the convoy, we were joined by 10 Hurricanes from No 615 Squadron and, to the west of us, nine Spitfires from No 610 Squadron were also flying their patrol at a higher altitude.

'Towards the end of our patrol, "Sapper" – out ground controller – warned us of enemy aircraft approaching from the southeast and sure

enough there they were – a force of at least 50 aircraft, comprised of Ju 87s escorted by Me 109s and Me 110s. Happily, we were "up sun" of them, and I think unseen. As the Ju 87s started their dive, "The Baron" led the six aircraft of Green and Red Sections down to bounce them. I was about to follow with Sub Lt Gordon Bulmer and Sgt Bill Higgins when I saw about 30 Me 109s taking an unwelcome interest in us, so I swung Blue Section around to attack them. This seemed to offend them so much that they picked on my section of three Hurricanes instead and from what had been a peaceful sky suddenly erupted into a confused melee of aircraft swirling round firing at anything in sight.

'One of the Messerschmitts overshot me and I managed more by luck than judgment to get on his tail. Opening fire in five-second bursts at a distance of 150 yards and closing, I had soon set the Me 109 on fire. This made me even more unpopular with his squadron mates and the excitement of the dogfight grew in intensity as four of them attacked me from different directions. I was not happy with such unfriendly attention, and made a head-on attack on two of them before running out of ammunition. As I wheeled round to guard my tail, I found that the sky had cleared and there was not an aircraft in sight – no friends, no foes, nothing. Feeling lonely and vulnerable, I made for home.'

No 32 Squadron had clashed with I./JG 51, Pete Brothers downing Oberfeldwebel Sicking of the Gruppe's 1. Staffel.

The Ju 87s continued to participate in the Kanalkampf despite increasing losses, which reached a head during this early phase of the Battle of Britain in a series of attacks on Convoy Peewit off the Isle of Wight on 8 August. Ten Stukas were lost. A survivor of the slaughter from II./StG 77 gave the following account of the convoy mission during a German radio broadcast:

'At the briefing we were told that our target was a British convoy trying to force the Channel route. We were given a code name for our attack – "Puma". We had no proper location and so we had to fly our mission most accurately by compass. Our wing leader had to give each squadron commander short and accurate instructions from what he knew, then everyone got dressed. The most important piece of clothing is the life jacket. Then, shortly before 16.00hrs, the whole group is ready, the first formation to take off being our commander's formation. A small signal lamp flashes and like a flock of large birds the squadrons rose up one after another into the sky. We all circle our base and collect information, then head off towards the Channel battleground. After

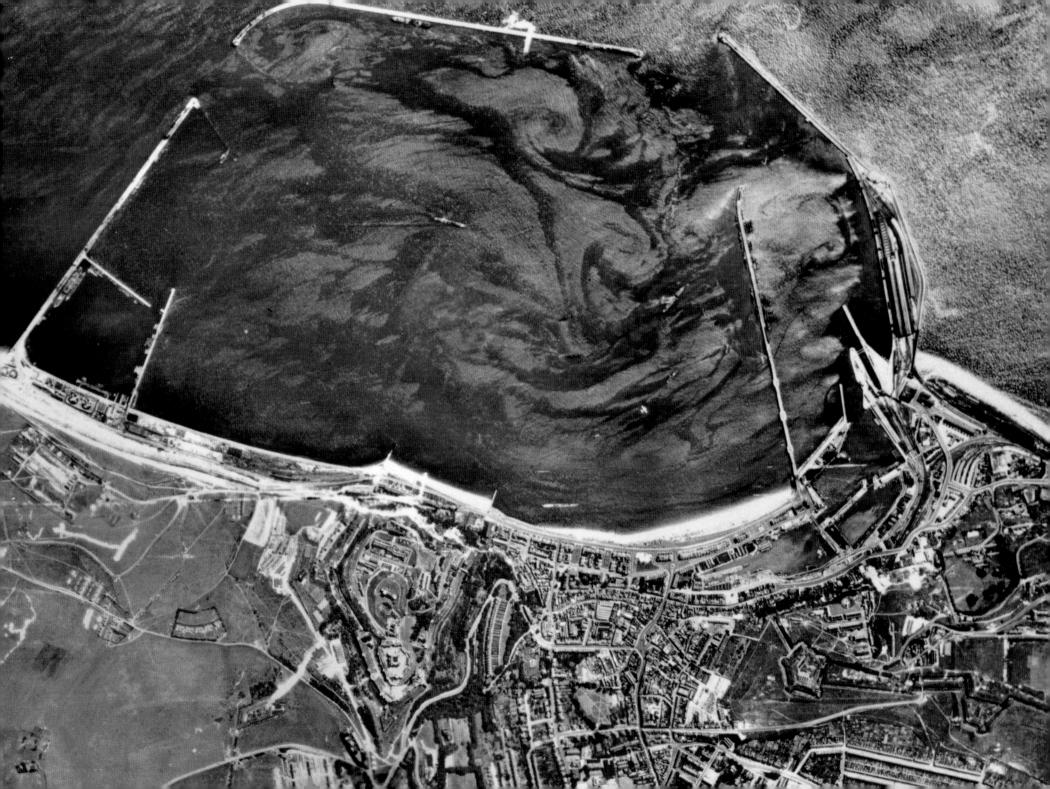

ACES *in* ART

'One of the Messerschmitts overshot me and I managed more by luck
than judgment to get on his tail.
Opening fire in five-second bursts at a distance of 150 yards and closing,
I had soon set the Me 109 on fire'

PETE BROTHERS

PETE BROTHERS

Flight Lieutenant

Lancastrian Pete Brothers learned to fly at 16 and joined the RAF in January 1937. Ten months later he was posted to No 32 Squadron at Biggin Hill and he was made a flight commander in late 1938. A vastly experienced pilot by the time he first saw action over France in May 1940, Brothers was in near continual action flying from Biggin Hill and Hawkinge during the summer of 1940. By the time he was posted to No 257 Squadron on 9 September, his score stood at 10 victories. Brothers duly claimed a Ju 88 and Do 17 destroyed on 15 September opposing the largest Luftwaffe raids of the Battle of Britain, these being his only successes with No 257 Squadron. Remaining in the fight throughout World War 2 with a series of operational postings, Brothers claimed further victories while leading Nos 457 and 602 Squadrons and the Tangmere and Culmhead Wings. Awarded a DFC and Bar and a DSO by war's end, Brothers' final victory tally was 16 destroyed and one probable.

Flying his personally modified Hurricane I N2921, Flt Lt Pete Brothers leads 'Blue Section' of No 32 Squadron as it heads out over the Channel.

Bomb racks empty, a trio of Ju 87Bs from Normandy-based 7./StG 77 return to Caen after attacking British vessels sailing off the south coast of England in early August 1940.

only a few minutes we are at the coast. Below us, as far as the eye can see, is the Channel. Once it was the busiest shipping lane in the world. Now it is the largest ships' graveyard.

'Water – nothing but water below us. We cannot see the coast or the enemy ships. Our thoughts are with our engines, those reliable humming helpers in our operation. Our eyes go from instrument to instrument, checking – water cooling, tachometer, pressure gauge – all of them are regularly checked. If our engine gives up there is only one thing left for us and that is to "ditch". The Channel is large and wide, and on the other side is the enemy island.

'There, carefully, one would like to say shyly, is a light strip emerging from the blue-green water. At first you can hardly make it out. The English south coast, and the white cliffs of the steep shore. A few hundred metres above us fly some squadrons of fighters – Me 109s and the long-range destroyer Me 110s – as protection for us. Half-right in front of us at about 3,000-4,000m the first air battle has already begun. You can hardly tell friend from enemy. We can only see small silver specks circling. Now we must be especially alert. The coast is getting nearer, to the left, below us, the Isle of Wight and we already see 10 or 12 ships. They, as they in turn spot us, try somehow to avoid our attacks by zig-zagging. We fly steadily eastwards towards them. Suddenly we hear through our R/T, "No 4 aircraft had crash-landed!" One of our 4. Staffel machines has had to go down into the water. His engine must have failed. We hope everything goes well for them as we press on.

"Puma 1 to all Pumas – Puma attack!" We are above the convoy. It all seems to be small ships, coasters. Our 1. Staffel has already started to attack. Now the formations pull apart. Each one of them chooses a ship that has not yet been hit by one of the other squadrons. Our Staffelkapitän's formation starts its attack dive near to the coast. But what is this? I cannot believe my eyes. There is a third formation that attacks with us in a dive from the left. At the same instant I hear "Puma – Alert. Enemy fighters diving from above!" When we are diving and banking vertically the English fighters have virtually no chance to shoot our Stukas, so they always try to intercept us earlier or catch us later on when we have pulled out of our dives. On account of them being so much faster than us, we always form up for mutual protection.

'That's for later. Right now I select my formation's target, which is the most southerly ship of the convoy. Before I commence my dive I make sure by asking my radio operator if everything is clear behind us.

I receive the reply "All clear!" Then we dive down without deploying the air brakes, as in our perilous position we need speed to get back into our unit formation again. My bombs land close alongside the ship, and my left-hand Kettenhund aircraft also scores a near miss by a very near margin, but the third aircraft of the formation hits the vessel square amidships with his bombs. Within seconds a huge flame shoots up from the ship and a large cloud of smoke bellows out of her insides. As we fly away, we can see her listing badly and on fire.

'Now the English defenders are right on top of us! Spitfires and Hurricanes. From a distance you cannot distinguish these from our own Me 109s. Above the Isle of Wight it makes for a terrible battle. About 60 aircraft of all makes, German and English, all fighting for their very lives. Some of the English draw back towards the coast of England, while on the left of me an Me 109 drops into the sea. The pilot is able to get out and slowly he guides his parachute towards the water. Another aircraft, the make I cannot see clearly, circles in flames like a bonfire above us. Then it explodes and falls in many small pieces. You can only recognise the engine compartment.

'When we all collect towards the south the English take us on. Only weaving helps you if you want to escape the eight machine guns of the English fighters. Our radio operators shoot whenever they can get their guns to bear. Again and again I feel bullets striking my aircraft but I don't think the engine has been hit. The motor is quiet and smooth. The closer we get to the centre of the English Channel the fewer English aircraft attack us. Our squadrons find each other bit by bit and we form up. To the left of us flies our 4. Staffel. One of the aeroplanes has a smoke trail behind it. The pilot gives the message "Aircraft damaged, going into the water!' At that moment a Spitfire comes in from ahead of us, shoots, and down into the water the damaged Stuka goes. But the Englishman does not live long to enjoy his cheap victory and glory. As he veers away after his attack, he gets hit by a Me 109 and dives vertically into the sea.

'After 30 minutes of flying, we at last see the coast of Normandy. We all sigh with relief. My formation comrades approach to the side of the aircraft, nod and smile. Everything in our squadron seems to be all right. We land at our base. Unbelievably, all of the aircraft from our Staffel have returned. Some have up to 40 bullet holes in their fuselage and wings, but all land despite this. Later, we learn that our commander, Hauptmann [Waldemar] Plewig, is missing [he survived

the ditching and was captured, but his radio operator. Fledwebel Kurt Schauer, perished]. We cannot believe it. Nobody saw the CO ditch.'

Kanalkampf reached its climax on 12 August with a series of bloody, and successful, pinpoint attacks on all known radar stations in an attempt to blind the RAF in preparation for the launching of phase two of the Battle of Britain on the 13th – Adlerangriff ('Attack of the Eagles'). However, of the four sites hit during the course of the day, three were operational within several hours. Despite having suffered high losses during the Channel battles (in just three weeks in July, 220 pilots had been shot down into the sea), Fighter Command was upbeat as its squadrons had made consistently high claims. Although some realised that these tallies were not strictly accurate, Dowding was in no doubt about the losses he had sustained. For the moment, however, these casualties had not significantly weakened Fighter Command's ability to wage an effective campaign against the Luftwaffe.

Between 29 June and 2 August, 322 Hurricanes and 166 Spitfires had been delivered to the RAF as fighter production vastly improved. These quantities more than covered the number of fighters damaged or destroyed prior to the start of the Kanalkampf, and Fighter Command now had more pilots to draw on – 1,456 at the end of July. Each and every one of these men, and more besides, would be needed in the next phase of the campaign.

NOTWT

ANY REPLY TO THIS MESSAGE
IS TO BE ENDORSED NOTWT

IMMEDIATE

FROM MANSTON

L.A.F. STATION, NORTH WEALD
13 JUL 1940
SIGNALS OFFICE

NWEALD

13/7/40

11 FIGHTER   NR21   IMMEDIATE - NOT - WT

PASS SELF   GR189

ADDRESSED TO HQ 16 GROUP RPT HORNCHURCH AND NORTH WEALD

FROM MANSTON

N1/2 13/7

PRELIMINARY AND COMPOSITE REPORT

FIVE A/C OF 56 SQUADRON LANDED AT MANSTON AT 1853 . 3 JU87

CLAIMED SHOT DOWN AND ONE ME109 . PATROLLING THE DOVER-DEAL COAST

THEY SIGHTED 12 JU87 APPROACHING DOVER FROM THE FRENCH COAST

AT 8000 FEET . A SQUADRON OF ME109 WAS ESCORTING ENEMY BOMBERS

APPROX 4000 FEET HIGHER, BUT OUR A/C SURPRISED ENEMY BOMBERS

AND BROKE UP FORMATION BEFORE FIGHTERS CAME DOWN . JU87'S

IMMEDIATELY TURNED FOR FRANCE WHEN ATTACKED AND THREE UNCONFIRMED

WERE SHOT DOWN . ONE PILOT OF 56 SQUADRON ALSO CLAIMED ONE ME10 .

UNCONFIRMED WHICH WAS COVERING THE RETREAT OF THE BOMBERS 10 MILES

FROM FRENCH COAST . ONE HURRICANE OF 56 SQUADRON WAS SEEN TO COME

DOWN IN THE SEA NECESSARY RESCUE ACTION TAKEN WITH FIGHTER COMMAND

ANOTHER FORCE LANDED NEAR KINGSDOWN BUT PILOT SGT BAKER

WAS UNHURT AND IS STANDING BY MACHINE . THE STATION HAS TAKEN

NECESSARY ACTION WITH REGARD TO A/C . FOUR OF THE 5 A/C LANDED

SERVICABLE ALL PILOTS SERVICABLE . FOUR A/C NOW RETURNING TO

NORTH WEALD ====1740

WA   THE SEA TO READ :- NECESSARY+ GEO VA +++

.TJ...VA+

SHQ
56 2yh.

OSKAR DINORT

Geschwaderkommodore

The first Stuka pilot to be awarded the Knight's Cross with Oak Leaves (in July 1941), Oskar Dinort was a natural aviator. Indeed, he set gliding world records and won flying competitions in Germany during the interwar period. Transferred from the Freikorps to the still secret Luftwaffe in 1934, Dinort flew biplane fighters until switching to dive-bombers in 1937. As Gruppenkommandeur of Ju87-equipped II./StG 2, he completed 40 missions during the Polish campaign. Promoted to Geschwaderkommodore of StG 2 in October 1939, Dinort led this unit in various theatres during two years of near-constant combat. His most successful action in the summer of 1940 was on 4 July when StG 2 attacked convoy OA 178 in the Channel and Portland harbour. Three ships were sunk and five damaged. After the Battle of Britain, Dinort and StG 2 fought in the Balkan and Crete campaigns, before being sent to the Eastern Front. Dinort, who took up a staff position after leaving StG 2 in October 1941, survived the war.

A Schwarm of Bf 109E-1/3s from 5./JG 26 are led on a patrol by Hauptmann Karl Ebbighausen in late June 1940. Ebbighausen had just claimed a Spitfire southwest of Dover for his 10th victory on 15 August when he was in turn shot down by Flt Lt Al Deere. His body was never found.

Split into two vics of three, six Hurricanes of No 56 Squadron practice a diving interception.

The combat report generated by No 56 Squadron's Intelligence Officer following action over the Channel against Ju 87s and Bf 109s (the latter from JG 51) on 13 July 1940.

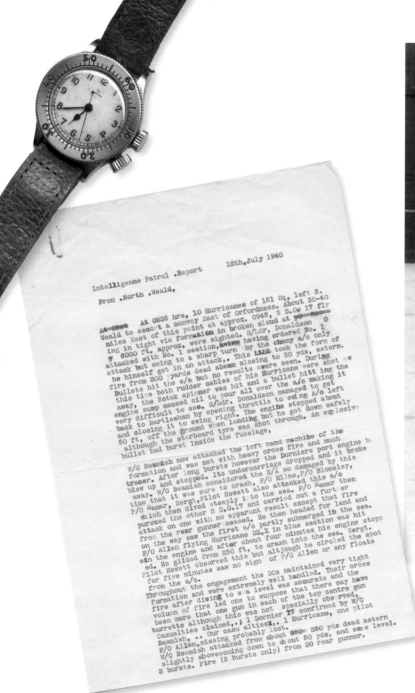

Intelligence Patrol .Report   12th,July 1940

From .North .Weald,

At 0835 hrs, 10 Hurricanes of 151 Sq, left N.
Weald to escort a convoy East of Orfordness. About 50-40
miles East of this point at approx. 0945, 5 D.O. 17 fly
ing in tight vic formation in broken cloud at 6000 ft. approx. were sighted. S/Ldr, Donaldson
attacked with No. 1 section, having ordered No. 1
he himself got in an attack. This took the form of
fire from 300 yards dead abeam closing to 50 yds, astern.
Bullets hit the e/a but no results were seen. During
this time both rudder cables of his Hurricane were shot
away, the Rotak spinner was hit and a bullet hitting the
engine sump caused oil to pour all over the a/c making it
very difficult to see. S/Ldr. Donaldson managed to get
back to Martlesham by opening throttle to swing about
and closing it to swing right. The engine stopped about
50 ft, off the ground when landing but he got down safely
although the starboard tyre was shot through. An explosive
bullet had burst inside the fuselage,

W/C Beamish now attacked the left hand machine of the
formation and was met with heavy cross fire and much
tracer. After long bursts however the Dorniers port engine b.
blew up and stopped. Its undercarriage dropped and it broke
away. W/C Beamish considered the E/A so damaged by this
time that it was sure to crash, P/O Milne, P/O Blomeley,
P/O Hamar, Sergt, Pilot Hewett also attacked this a/c
which then dived steeply into the sea. P/O Hamar then
pursued the other 2 D.O.17 and carried out a further
attack on one with no apparant result except that fire
from the rear gunner ceased. He then headed for land and
on the way saw the first a/c partly submerged in the sea.
P/O Allen flying Hurricane DZ,K in blue section was hit
in the engine and after about four minutes his engine stopp
ed. He glided from 250 ft, to crash into the spot
Pilot Hewett observed this but altjough he circled the spot
for five minutes saw no sign of P/O Allen or any floats
from the a/c.

Throughout the engagement the DOs maintained very tight
formation and were extremely well handled. Their cross
fire after diving to s a level was accurate and the
volume of fire led one to suppose that there may have
been more that one gun in each of the top centre gun
turrets although this was not specially observed,

Casualties claimed, . 1 Dornier 17 confirmed by W/O
Beamish, .. Our casualties.. 1 Hurricane, one pilot
P/O Allen,missing probably lost. .. 250 yds dead astern
W/C Beamish attacked from about 50 yds, and same level.
slightly abovecoming down to about 50 yds, and same level.
3 bursts. Fire (2 bursts only) from DO rear gunner.

On 27 June 1940, HM George VI visited Hornchurch to present decorations to five pilots who had enjoyed success over the evacuation beaches. Having received their medals, Plt Off J. L. Allen (DFC), Flt Lt R. R. Stanford Tuck (DFC), Flt Lt A. C. Deere (DFC), Flt Lt A. G. Malan (DFC) and Sqn Ldr J. A. Leathart (DSO) give the King a hearty three cheers. Only Johnny Allen failed to survive the war, being killed on 24 July 1940 when he stalled in near Cliftonville while trying to force land his shot up Spitfire.

Bombs explode within the waters of Dover harbour during the early morning raid of 29 July 1940 by 48 Ju 87s escorted by around 80 Bf 109s. Three vessels were sunk for the loss of four Stukas.

A dramatic photograph from Der Adler taken by a Do 17Z during a Kanalkampf mission against an unidentified harbour target.

'Within seconds a huge flame shoots up from the ship and a large cloud of smoke bellows out of her insides. As we fly away, we can see her listing badly and on fire.'

STUKA PILOT

Bomben auf England!　　　　VERLAG ERICH KLINGHAMMER · BERLIN

Clearly approaching the English coast, the crew of a Ju 88 scan the skies ahead for signs of Spitfires and Hurricanes.

The Ju 88A-1 could carry a maximum bomb load of 4,409lb split between the bomb-bay and underwing racks – ordnance is seen here being shackled to the latter with the help of a dedicated bomb dolly.

This Ju 88A-1 of Stab II./KG 54 was force-landed by its crew on 11 August 1940 after the pilot of the bomber was badly wounded in an attack by a Spitfire at 9,000ft during an attempted raid on Portland harbour. Oberleutnant K. Wette brought the aircraft down near Blacknor Fort. The censor was keen to obliterate the recognisable background to this photograph prior to clearing it for release to the press.

Attacked by Hurricanes of No 43 Squadron as it came over the Isle of Wight and Southampton Water, this He 111P of Stab/KG 55 belly-landed near the Horse and Jockey Inn in Hipley at 16.30hrs. Of the five-man crew, three were wounded in the attack.

Two Bf 110Cs from 6./ZG 2 flying brazenly along the white cliffs of England's south coast. This famous propaganda photograph was released at the height of the Battle of Britain.

The two-man crew of a Bf 110C during a Channel sweep in the summer of 1940.

'Our eyes go from instrument to instrument, checking – water cooling, tachometer, pressure gauge – all of them are regularly checked. If our engine gives up there is only one thing left for us and that is to "ditch". The Channel is large and wide, and on the other side is the enemy island'

LUFTWAFFE PILOT

ROYAL AIR FORCE

No. 32 SQN
Photo Diary

"... 'Borough of Grimstone' calling 'Metal-Workers' Guild' and 'Ethels of the Empire.'"

Three Hurricanes from No 32 Squadron return to Biggin Hill on 15 August 1940 after intercepting waves of bombers.

A smiling 'B' Flight commander and ace, Flt Lt Pete Brothers.

Plt Off Douglas 'Grubby' Grice, who claimed five victories and one unconfirmed destroyed.

Overleaf:
No 32 Squadron's officer cadre in July 1940. Standing, from left to right, are Plt Off J. P. Pfeiffer, Flt Lt J. B. W. Humpherson, Plt Off P. M. Gardner, Sqn Ldr M. N. Crossley and Plt Offs D. H. Grice and J. F. Pain. Seated, from left to right, are Plt Offs A. K. Eckford, K. Pniak and B. A. Wlasnowski.

Pilots relax at their Hawkinge dispersal on 29 July 1940. From left to right, Plt Offs R. F. Smythe, K. R. Gillman and J. E. Proctor, Flt Lt P. M. Brothers and Plt Offs D. H. Grice, P. M. Gardner and A. F. Eckford. All survived the Battle of Britain and the war as aces, bar Keith Gillman, who was posted missing in action on 25 August 1940.

Plt Off Keith Gillman, who was posted missing in action on 25 August 1940. This photograph subsequently featured on the cover of numerous publications.

Pilots of 'A' Flight scramble for their Hurricanes on 12 August.

Plt Off Smythe prepares to take off from the dispersal area at Hawkinge in P3522, having received the order to scramble to intercept an incoming raid by Ju 88s and He 111s.

Plt Off Gardner tries to catch up on his sleep at Hawkinge on 29 July. By the end of the battle, Gardner's tally stood at seven confirmed victories and two damaged.

PICTURE POST

THE MEN AGAINST GOERING

HULTONS NATIONAL WEEKLY   SHOULD EUROPE STARVE? 3ᴰ

PHASE TWO

Target - Fighter Command

....

"Cry Havoc and
let Slip the
Dogs of War"

Julius Caesar, Act III, Scene I

William Shakespeare

Attack of Eagles

Although the primary German objective – mastery of the skies over England – had still to be achieved, Hitler had issued Führer-Direktiv No 17 on 1 August that authorised Göring to launch a major attack on Britain at his convenience after 5 August. The heart of the British defences was now to become the target. Massive formations of bombers, closely escorted by fighters, were to blast fighter airfields, radar installations and aircraft factories. Dubbed the Adlerangriff, the 'Attack of Eagles' was to be the onslaught that was supposed to mark the beginning of the end of British air defences and set the stage for the invasion in September. Assured by his Air Fleet commanders that Fighter Command was reeling, Göring was convinced that the RAF would be crippled within four weeks.

The offensive did not get off to the best of starts, with poor weather forcing Göring to postpone the morning attacks of Adlertag. Conditions improved in the afternoon, and by nightfall the Luftwaffe had flown an unprecedented 1,485 sorties over England – many of them by Bf 109s performing 'freie jagd' sweeps ahead of the bombers. By now, however, Fighter Command's controllers were getting the measure of these 'free sweeps', refusing to commit precious fighters to engage them. As a direct result of this, only 700 sorties were flown against the Luftwaffe on 13 August, whereas on many days in July, far smaller raids by the Germans had seen 600 or more sorties generated.

Forty-eight hours later the Luftwaffe mounted the largest number of sorties of the campaign, flying 1,786 missions in what became known as 'The Greatest Day'. Luftflotte 5 made a rare appearance in strength over northern England that day, 65 He 111s and 50 Ju 88s from bases in Scandinavia expecting to attack targets with little opposition as the Luftwaffe believed most of Fighter Command's strength was in the south. The bombers' escort of 34 Bf 110s proved to be woefully inadequate, with 16 bombers and seven fighters being destroyed. Spitfire-equipped No 72 Squadron was in the thick of the action, as Plt Off Robert Deacon-Elliott subsequently recalled:

'We were sent off from Acklington up in Yorkshire to patrol at Angels 24 [24,000ft], east of the Farne Islands, off the coast in the North Sea.

We intercepted a raid of at least 150 aircraft coming to bomb the north of England while others were attacking down south. Every type of German aeroplane we knew was there. We'd never seen anything like it before [No 72 Squadron had rarely encountered the Luftwaffe up to that point in the war]. During our training, we'd learned to do "Number One Attack", "Number Two Attack", "Number Three Attack" etc. – you knew exactly what each of these meant. So someone called out to our acting squadron commander, Ted Graham, "Have you seen them?" Ted, who stuttered, replied, "Of course I've seen the b-b-bastards. I'm trying to w-w-work out wh-wh-what to do." But we already were about to reach them.

'Graham hurtled in through the gap between the bombers and their escort, and each of us picked a target. I saw two Huns literally disintegrate. The bombers quickly began jettisoning their loads. The sea below churned up white with bombs as if a colony of whales was spouting. We hacked them about so badly the formation split apart and they made for home. That was the first and last time formations of Germans came over the North Sea by day.'

15 August proved to be disastrous for the Luftwaffe, which had 71 aircraft destroyed as crews pressed home their attacks with courage and determination – the RAF lost 29 aeroplanes in return. Only eight of the German aircraft destroyed were Bf 109s, reinforcing Fighter Command's stated policy of targeting bombers first and foremost. From then on, the Luftwaffe would only commit the proportion of its bomber strength for which fighter cover was available.

The following day a further 1,700 sorties were flown by Luftflotten 2 and 3, and for the first time British pilots reported meeting Bf 109s flying close escort to German bomber formations rather than free-ranging top cover. However, the German fighters could not stop nine Ju 87s being shot down during attacks on Manston, Harwell, Farnborough, Lee-on-Solent and Tangmere, although the Stukas inflicted considerable damage on their targets. No 602 Squadron was flying from Tangmere's nearby satellite when the sector station was hit, the unit's CO, Sqn Ldr Sandy Johnstone, recalling:

'It was as we sat down for lunch that the fun and games started. The phone went and we were told, "Get airborne!" It wasn't "Come to readiness", or anything nice and calm like that. We had been given the order to scramble from a "Released" state, and the reason became all too apparent as we rushed helter-skelter from the Mess to see 30 Ju 87 dive-bombers screaming vertically down on Tangmere. The noise was terrifying as the explosion of the bombs mingled with the din of ack-ack guns, which were firing from positions all around us. We could hear the rattle of spent bullets as they fell on the metal-covered Nissen huts where we hurriedly donned our flying kit. Chunks of spent lead fell about us as we jinked our way to our parked aircraft. Our crews, wearing steel helmets, had already started the engines and sped us on our way with the minimum of delay. It was a complete panic take-off, with Spitfires darting together from all corners of the field, and it was a miracle that none collided in the frantic scramble to get airborne.

'I called the boys to form up over base at Angels 2 [2,000ft]. A Flight was already with me, but there was no sign of B Flight. However, there was no time to stop and look for them! The air was a kaleidoscope of aeroplanes swooping and diving around us and for a moment I felt like pulling the blankets over my head and pretending I wasn't there! I had no idea it could be as chaotic as this. A Hurricane on fire flashed past me and I was momentarily taken aback when the pilot of the aircraft in front of me baled out. Then, it was all over. No one else was about.

'Boyd, Urie, McDowall and myself all claimed victories. I think Boyd's effort was the best of the bunch, for a Stuka pulled out of its dive right in front of him just as he became airborne and when he pressed his firing button it simply blew apart. He said that he was so surprised he merely completed a circuit and landed, without even retracting his landing gear! I don't suppose he had been airborne for more than a couple of minutes.

'I drove over to Tangmere in the evening and found the place an utter shambles, with wisps of smoke still rising from the shattered buildings. Little knots of people were wandering about with dazed looks on their faces, obviously deeply affected by the events of the day. I eventually tracked down the station commander [Grp Capt Jack Boret], standing on the lawn in front of the officer's mess with a parrot sitting on his shoulder. Jack was covered with grime and the wretched bird was screeching its imitation of the Stuka at the height of the attack!'

Despite the Luftwaffe having suffered high losses since it launched Adlerangriff, its High Command was convinced that Fighter Command was now down to just 300 serviceable aircraft. Poor intelligence such as this let the Germans down badly throughout the campaign, as in reality the RAF had three times that number. Buoyed by the misleading figures, Kesselring and Sperrle planned a series of ambitious raids for 18 August that would see Kenley, Biggin Hill, Hornchurch, North Weald and targets around Portsmouth hit hard. The most daring attack of the day was undertaken by nine Do 17Zs of 9./KG 76, which carried out a low-altitude raid on the No 11 Group airfield at Kenley, in Surrey, as part of a complex pincer attack on the sector station by KG 76 as a whole.

A very stable aircraft at low-level, the Do 17 was ideally suited to such a mission. As the Staffel raced across the Channel in line abreast formation towards the Sussex coast west of Beachy Head, the nine bombers left wakes across the surface of the sea with their propeller slipstreams. 'We zoomed over the English countryside, a few metres high', wrote Rolf von Pebal, who was one of eight reporters and photographers of the 4th Reporter Detachment to fly with KG 76 on this mission. Every fold in the ground served as cover for us, each wood was exploited as a hiding place. We bounded over trees, undulating the whole time. A train rushed by underneath us. A couple of cyclists dashed for cover in a ditch by the side of the road'.

Having been spotted by the Observer Corps as the formation approached the south coast, the Dorniers of 9. Staffel were duly intercepted by Hurricanes from Croydon-based No 111 Squadron as the bombers closed on Kenley. One of the pilots involved was Plt Off Ronald Brown:

'We picked them up 10 miles from Kenley. I had just got into firing range and I got a long burst in at the leader of their sections when he broke formation and pulled up. I was damn certain that I must have hit him, but just at that moment, as we were about to cross the airfield, the airfield defence system went into action. Rockets fired wires and parachutes into the air. I had heard of these things but I had never seen them before and I damn near hit them. I went up fast to avoid them. In the meantime bombs were bursting below us. I got over the other side of the airfield and picked up another Dornier, which was right down in the valley. I got in a good long burst on his starboard quarter and down he went. He burnt up in a field. I saw another one going over a housing estate. I was about to fire at him but at that moment I visualised a woman and kids in their kitchen cooking the Sunday lunch. So I sat behind this fellow for quite a long time while his rear gunner popped off at me. When he was clear of the estate I took a burst at him but that was my third attack and by now I was out of ammo. I don't know if he got home.'

Three Do 17Zs of 9./KG 76 approach Beachy Head at 13.00hrs on 18 August en route to RAF Kenley during the unit's daring low-level raid.

Unteroffizier Günther Unger was flying the Do 17 furthest to the left in the nine-bomber formation:

'The hail of light flak and machine gun fire showered around us, the red points of the tracer flying by. I pushed the aircraft yet lower and went in exactly over the left-hand hangars'.

Unteroffizier Schumacher was flying an aeroplane on the right side of the formation:

'Bombs were bouncing down the runway like rubber balls. Hell was let loose. Then the bombs began their work of destruction. Three hangars collapsed like matchwood. Explosions followed explosions, flames leapt into the sky. It seemed as if my aircraft was grabbed by some giant. Bits of metal and stones clattered against the fuselage, something thudded into my back armour and splinters of glass flew. There was a smell of phosphorus and smouldering cables.'

War reporter Georg Hinze was in the Do 17 flown by Oberleutnant Hermann Magin, which was leading the right-hand section of three:

'Suddenly the pilot slumped forward and cried "Nach Hause!" (take me home!). A bullet had hit him squarely in the chest. His left hand fell from the control column, dripping blood. The navigator leaned over the unconscious pilot and grabbed the control column, shouting the preparatory order "Prepare to jump!" to the rest of us.'

Feldwebel Stephani was flying the Do 17 to the right of Magin's bomber, and he recalled 'the aircraft in front of me went into a tight turn to the right, the formation split up and it was every man for himself'. Feldwebel Wilhelm Raab, in the lead section, was passing over the airfield when 'suddenly red-glowing balls rose up from the ground in front of me. Each one trailed a line of smoke about one metre thick behind it, with intervals of 10 to 15 metres between each. I had experienced machine gun and flak fire often enough, but this was something entirely new. Everything seemed to be going well – then I felt a hefty tug on my machine. "Now they've got us", I thought. "We are going to be smashed into the ground".'

Somehow the Do 17 escaped from the parachutes and cables, Raab keeping it down close to the ground as he raced for the Channel. He was pursued by Hurricanes, however. 'To the rear I fired magazine after magazine at the fighters', explained radio operator Unteroffizier Erich Malter. 'My steel helmet fell off and I had no time to put it back on again. We were all sweating like bulls. The machine rushed on just above the surface of the ground. The fighters did not let up. At first

they came from behind, then, on my fire, they separated and positioned themselves to the left and the right behind our machine. First, the left one attacked. I had a jam and had to watch as the fighter came in to 20-30 metres. Then I cleared the stoppage and fired like mad at him.'

Eventually, the surviving Do 17s reached the Channel, but their problems were far from over. 'We left the English coast and joyful expressions appeared on all faces, but the battle was not yet over', Unteroffizier Schumacher explained. 'The left motor began to give up, visibly losing revolutions. A long line of black smoke trailed behind us. The speed fell and unfortunately I had no way of knowing what it was because the airspeed indicator was shot to pieces. Suddenly, a shudder went through the aircraft and it appeared that it was about to break up. I switched off the ignition to the defective motor and the machine began to sink slowly. I tried to open the throttle to the right motor but the lever was already hard against the stop.' The pilot told the crew to prepare for ditching, and although Schumacher set the bomber down as gently as possible, there was a Force 4 sea running and the water smashed in the Dornier's perspex nose. All four crewmen got out, although the flight engineer subsequently drowned.

Of the nine Do 17s that had attacked Kenley at just 100ft, two had been shot down near their target, two more crashed into the Channel on their way home due to battle damage and three force-landed in France. Just two Dorniers made it safely back to base, one of which was flown by navigator Wilhelm-Friedrich Illg after his pilot, Oberleutnant Hermann Magin, had succumbed to his wounds. Of the 40 men on board the aircraft, eight had been killed, five taken prisoner, three returned with wounds and seven had ditched in the Channel.

That same day no fewer than 19 Ju 87s were destroyed in raids on the south coast, thus forcing the Luftwaffe to remove the aircraft permanently from the action on the Channel Front. The Stukageschwader had recorded losses of 39 aircraft in 14 raids during the course of just two weeks. With Luftflotten 2, 3 and 5 having suffered terrible casualties during the early stages of Adlerangriff (403 German aircraft were lost between 13 and 23 August, compared to 175 RAF fighters) a relative lull in the fighting was observed from 19 through to 23 August. It would resume again with a vengeance on the 24th as Göring ordered his bombers to destroy Fighter Command by concentrating on its airfields.

The next phase of the battle was about to begin...

Although the Do 17Z had a performance advantage at low altitude over other German bombers, this was negated when the Luftwaffe switched to attacking London with large formations at medium altitude.

THE NIGHTMARE OF GOERING

Daily Mirror, London.

Pilots from an unidentified squadron in No 11 Group try and relax between sorties in early August. With the onset of Adlerangriff, however, there was little time available for games.

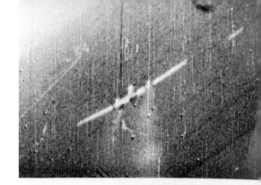

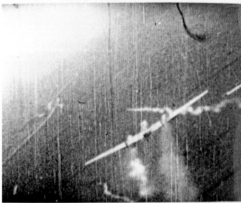

He 111Ps sit in a large hangar somewhere in France, awaiting preparation for their next mission to England, August 1940. Parked between them is a Bf 108 liaison aircraft.

Fearsome 'Sharksmouth' Zerstörer of II.ZG 76's. Staffel patrolling off the French coast, August 1940.

A Bf 110 is dispatched by a Hurricane over the Channel during the Battle of Britain, the 'kill' being recorded by the fighter's gun camera.

HANS-JOACHIM JABS

Oberleutnant

Having joined the Luftwaffe in 1935, Hans-Joachim Jabs originally served as a bomber pilot before switching to fighters (initially the Bf 109). He was transferred to Bf 110C-equipped II./ZG 76 at Cologne-Wahn in March 1940. Finding himself in the thick of the action from the very start of the Blitzkrieg, Jabs claimed a French Hawk 75 destroyed on 12 May. By the end of the Battle of France his tally stood at six victories, all of which were fighters. Jabs claimed a Spitfire and a Hurricane during the bloody clashes of 15 August and by the time he was awarded the Knight's Cross and promotion to Oberleutnant on 1 October 1940, his tally stood at 20 (including eight Spitfires and five Hurricanes). Retraining in late 1941 as a nightfighter pilot, Jabs' final successes came on the night of 21 February 1945 when he downed two Lancasters to take his tally to 50 victories – 22 day and 28 night kills. One of the highest-scoring Bf 110 aces to survive the war, Jabs had completed 710 missions by VE Day.

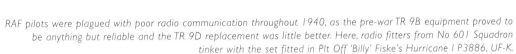

RAF pilots were plagued with poor radio communication throughout 1940, as the pre-war TR 9B equipment proved to be anything but reliable and the TR 9D replacement was little better. Here, radio fitters from No 601 Squadron tinker with the set fitted in Plt Off 'Billy' Fiske's Hurricane I P3886, UF-K.

'He died for England'. William Meade Lindsley 'Billy' Fiske was the first American serving with Fighter Command to be killed during the Battle of Britain. A wealthy stockbroker, film producer and Olympic medallist, as well as the husband of the former Countess of Warwick, Fiske joined No 601 Squadron in July 1940 having never flown a Hurricane before. Effectively trained 'on the job', he proved to be a gifted fighter pilot and saw near-daily action from 20 July through to his death on 17 August from wounds he had received in combat defending RAF Tangmere the previous day. 'Billy' Fiske is buried at Bromsgrove Priory, near Tangmere.

Airfield Attacks

From 24 August through to 6 September the battle entered its deadliest phase for Fighter Command, as Göring ordered his units to fly concentrated attacks on the No 11 Group airfields. In truth, the strategic direction of the air campaign remained the same. Now, however, the Luftwaffe would prosecute its raids with greater skill and better tactics, using its strength in numbers to attempt a breakthrough of the defences in daylight that it hoped would force the RAF to abandon its airfields in the extreme south and southeast. Factories supporting the British aircraft industry were to be attacked as well.

Raids were now mounted with such frequency that Operations Rooms Controllers had difficulty determining which deserved priority attention from the limited defence resources now at their disposal. It was now routine to send sections of three aircraft or flights of six to intercept formations of up to 100 or more attacking aeroplanes. Such extreme odds led to mounting casualties in Fighter Command and by early September few squadrons in No 11 Group had enough men to put 12 fighters into the air. Although the third phase of the campaign lasted just 14 days, it was during this period that British defences came closest to collapse.

'A fresh squadron coming into an active sector would generally bring with them 16 aircraft and about 20 trained pilots', recalled Air Chief Marshal Dowding. 'They would normally fight until they were no longer capable of putting more than nine aircraft into the air and then they had to be relieved. This process occupied different periods according to the luck and the skill of the unit. The normal period was a month to six weeks, but some units had to be replaced after a week or 10 days. By the beginning of September, the incidence of casualties became so serious that a fresh squadron would become depleted and exhausted before any of the resting and reforming squadrons was ready to take its place. Fighter pilots still could not be turned out by the training units in numbers sufficient to fill the widening gaps in the fighting ranks. Transfers were made from the Fleet Air Arm and from Bomber and Coastal Commands, but these pilots naturally required a short flying course on Hurricanes and Spitfires'.

Dowding had used the brief lull caused by poor weather after 18 August to add four new foreign-manned squadrons to Fighter Command's frontline strength, with Polish, Czech and Royal Canadian Air Force units all now being declared operational before month-end. Of the 3,080 aircrew who fought in the Battle of Britain, about 20 per cent of them were not British – 537 pilots from 13 different nations saw combat with Fighter Command. Hundreds of men were from countries in Europe that had fallen under Nazi domination, while volunteers from across the British Empire also made their way to Britain to join the air war. There were of course a number of Australian, Canadian, New Zealand and South African pilots already serving as short commission officers in Fighter Command when war started in 1939.

No fewer than 147 Poles flew with the RAF in 1940 and they made the greatest contribution to Fighter Command. They deeply resented the fact that their air force had been wiped out within the first few days of the German invasion in September 1939. Noted military historian and novelist Len Deighton described them as 'homeless men, motivated often by a hatred bordering upon despair, who fought with a terrible and merciless dedication'. In the main, the Polish aviators were more highly-trained than British pilots of the period, although they had no experience of high-performance monoplanes. They were, however, crack marksmen. Most Polish pilots spoke no English, so they were initially given British squadron and flight commanders to lead them alongside their own officers. Finally declared operational in late August due to Fighter Command's growing shortage of pilots, their scoring rate proved to be phenomenal. Indeed, in September No 303 'Polish' Squadron achieved the highest kill rate in Fighter Command. Overall, this unit, and Polish-manned No 302 Squadron, contributed 7.5 per cent of Fighter Command's entire total of enemy aircraft destroyed, despite missing the first seven weeks of the campaign. The Poles had 'swung into the fight with a dash of enthusiasm which is beyond praise', wrote Dowding. 'They were inspired by a burning hatred of the Germans, which made them deadly opponents'.

Unfortunately for Fighter Command, not all the reinforcements being sent into action were as experienced as the Poles, as Flt Lt Al Deere of Hornchurch-based No 54 Squadron discovered during the unit's final spell in No 11 Group in early September:

'Our morale was getting a bit low because there were only three of us – George Gribble, Colin Gray and me – left in the squadron who had any combat experience. We had been there the whole time and were pretty tired. Each time we went up, there seemed to be more and more Germans up there. We'd gone through two squadron commanders. The new pilots who came in – they just went up and came down! You'd say to them, "Now, look, don't get yourself lost. Stick with us. Don't bother about shooting to start with". But, of course, they couldn't resist peeling off, and some of them didn't come back.

'One day, the adjutant rang me up and said, "There are two new pilots reporting to No 54 Squadron". I said, "Thank God. Send them over". They turned out to be two New Zealanders, like me, who'd been three months at sea coming over. They'd only flown Vildebeests, a very old-fashioned biplane, in training. They'd been sent to an operational conversion unit and given five or six hours on Spitfires. And that was it! They hadn't even seen a reflector sight. They both got shot down the second day and were fished out of the Channel and ended up in hospital together.'

Fatigue was affecting many of the pilots in No 11 Group, especially those like Sqn Ldr Peter Townsend of No 85 Squadron, based at Croydon airport, who had been in action since the Battle of France:

'Our dispersal point, with groundcrew and pilots' rest rooms, was in a row of villas on the airfield's western boundary. Invariably, I slept there half-clothed to be on the spot if anything happened. In the small hours of 24 August it did. The shrill scream and the deafening crash of bombs shattered my sleep. In the doorway young [Pyers Arthur] Worrall, a new arrival, was yelling something and waving his arms. Normally as frightened as anyone, not even bombs could move me then. I placed my pillow reverently over my head and waited for the rest. Worall still had the energy to be frightened. I was past caring. It was a bad sign. I was more exhausted than I realised.'

Fatigue not withstanding, Townsend subsequently claimed six German fighters destroyed in just four days between 28 and 31 August. He was himself forced to bale out with a foot wound after his Hurricane was shot up by a Bf 110 over Tunbridge Wells on the latter date.

Despite the best efforts of men like Peter Townsend and Al Deere, the Luftwaffe was inflicting serious damage on the vital sector stations and exacting an increasing toll on the RAF. 'This period 24 August to 6 September seriously drained the strength of Fighter Command as a whole', Prime Minister Winston Churchill noted in his six-volume history The Second World War. 'The Command lost in this fortnight 103 pilots killed and 128 seriously wounded, while 466 Spitfires and Hurricanes had been destroyed or damaged. Out of a total pilot strength of 1,000, nearly a quarter had been lost. Their places could only be filled by 260 new, ardent but inexperienced pilots drawn from training units, in many cases before their full courses were complete'.

Possibly worse still, Fighter Command's intricate and so far highly effective fighter defence, based around No 11 Group's sector stations, was now being repeatedly hit hard by nearly daily attacks from Luftflotten 2 and 3. Although it was not obvious to either side, the Luftwaffe was slowly achieving air superiority over southern England. The RAF continued to inflict significant casualties on German fighters and bombers, but the Luftwaffe still had ample reserves. Fighter Command, on the other hand, was struggling to replace both. Airfields and aircraft factories were now being bombed time after time as German bombers exploited growing gaps in the fighter cover.

'The enemy's bombing attacks by day did extensive damage to five of our forward aerodromes and also six of our seven Sector Stations', recalled Air Vice Marshal Park in 1941. 'There was a critical period between 28 August and 5 September when the damage to sector stations and our ground organisation was having a serious effect on the fighting efficiency of the fighter squadrons, who could not be given the same good technical and administrative services as previously. The absence of many essential telephone lines, the use of scratch equipment in emergency operations rooms and the general dislocation of ground organisations was seriously felt for about a week in the handling of squadrons by day to meet the enemy's massed attacks, which continued without the occasional break for a day, as had previously been the case. Biggin Hill was so severely damaged that only one squadron could operate from there, and the remaining two squadrons had to be placed under the control of adjacent sectors for over a week. Had the enemy intensified its heavy attacks against the adjacent sectors and knocked out their operations rooms or telephone communications, the fighter defences of London would have been in a parlous state during the last critical phase when heavy attacks were directed against the capital'.

Biggin Hill was particularly badly bombed in a series of raids. Bowser driver Aircraftsman Second Class Albert Hargraves witnessed the devastating attack on 30 August:

'It was a Sunday, around teatime. We had just come out of the canteen. The station commander announced over the tannoy that

Bomb craters scar the ground surrounding the critically important Chain Home towers of the Dover radar station, which was attacked – unsuccessfully – by Ju 87s on several occasions.

Ju 87Bs of III./StG 77 bombed the Poling radar site on 18 August, separate formations targeting the transmitter and receiver sites – one of the receiver towers was knocked down.

An unexploded bomb from a Luftwaffe raid is detonated at RAF Hemswell, Lincolnshire, on 27 August 1940.

The Chain Home station at Poling, in Sussex. On the left are the 360ft steel transmitter towers, with the 240ft wooden receiver towers on the right.

ALEXANDER GLÄSER

Kettenführer

'Alex' Gläser joined the Luftwaffe shortly after its existence was announced to the world in 1935. Hand-picked to flying Ju 87s, he saw early combat with I./StG 77 during the invasion of Poland in September 1939. A veteran of combat in France, Gläser had been promoted to Kettenführer by the time he participated in the Battle of Britain. Subsequently fighting in the Balkans in 1941 and then on the Eastern Front, Gläser received the Knight's Cross in February 1943 and the Oak Leaves in March 1945. Having risen through the ranks to become Gruppenkommandeur of II./StG 77 in April 1943, he remained in this position when the unit was re-equipped with Fw 190s in 1944 and became III./SG 10, before switching to command II./SG 77. By war's end Gläser had flown 1,123 missions (600 of them in the Ju 87), having seen action from the first day of the war to the last.

The reluctant celebrity. Kiwi ace Flt Lt Al Deere of No 54 Squadron is greeted enthusiastically by female workers at the HMV Gramophone Factory in London shortly after the Battle of Britain had ended.

Restored Spitfire IA X4650 is marked up in the colours it wore on 28 December 1940 when it was involved in a collision with Spitfire IA X4276, flown by Flt Lt Al Deere. Both the pilot of X4650, Sgt Howard Squire, and Al Deere took to their parachutes. The remains of X4650 were recovered from farmland in Cleveland in the 1970s and the fighter was subsequently restored to airworthiness.

everybody who wasn't essential should go to the shelters, but so many dashed for them that not everybody could get in. I dashed back to my bowser to drive to where there were some trees for cover. I'd just got onto the perimeter when the Dorniers came down the middle of the aerodrome – they came in with the sun at the back of them. They looked like they were only 50ft off the ground, though they must have been higher than that.

'The cab doors of the bowser had been taken off to let us get in and out in a hurry. I pulled up sharp, jumped out and ran like bloody hell to a hedge and lay down. The bombs were exploding and you could hear the machine guns and cannon fire from the Dorniers and Messerschmitts. Then it went quiet. The main shelter, the one where not everybody could get in, had been hit. There was a hell of a crater there. We rushed over and tried to get people out. There were a lot of casualties. There were heads lying around and arms sticking up out of the crater. We were digging away there until three in the morning. We got about 50 bodies out and there were still some left. The next day they got a load of miners in to help dig the shelter out. They found some more bodies. After they thought they'd got out as many as they could, they just bulldozed the area over.'

The attacks on the airfields in late August had brought friction to a head between Air Vice-Marshal Keith Park and Air Vice-Marshal Trafford Leigh-Mallory, his opposite number in No 12 Group. 'On a few dozen occasions when I had sent every available squadron of No 11 Group to engage the main enemy attack as far forward as possible, I called on No 12 Group to send a couple of squadrons to defend a fighter airfield or other vital targets which was threatened by outflanking and smaller bomber raids', Air Vice-Marshal Park recalled. 'Instead of sending two squadrons quickly to protect the vital targets, No 12 Group delayed while they dispatched a large wing of four or five squadrons, which wasted valuable time. Consequently, they invariably arrived too late to prevent the enemy bombing the target. On scores of days I called No 10 Group on my right for a few squadrons to protect some vital target. Never on any occasion can I remember this Group failing to send its squadrons promptly to the place requested, thus saving thousands of civilian lives and also the naval dockyards of Portsmouth, the port of Southampton and aircraft factories'.

No 601 Squadron ace Flt Lt Sir Archibald Hope explains how the Big Wing was supposed to work:

'The theory of the Big Wing was, if you had a raid of say 50 109s coming in with a lot of bombers below it, one of our squadrons of 12 aircraft couldn't do very much against them. You might shoot down a couple of the bombers, but you couldn't really stop the raid. However – so the theory went – if you had 24 or more aircraft up there, you'd stand a better chance of stopping it. But Leigh-Mallory and Douglas Bader were absolutely wrong about the Big Wings. He hadn't got enough squadrons. He had to get his aircraft airborne as quickly as he damn well could, in such numbers as he could.'

'Aside from that, Leigh-Mallory and Keith Park hated each other's guts. They couldn't stand each other. If one said it was the right way to do something, the other would be quite certain to say it was the wrong way.'

Sqn Ldr Tom Gleave, who led Hurricane-equipped No 253 Squadron until he suffered terrible burns baling out of an aircraft on 31 August, was also critical of the Big Wings:

'Apart from the fact that we didn't have enough aircraft to keep putting a Big Wing aloft, there was the question of the time it took. If you wanted to send one squadron, it took 14 minutes for it to get to 20,000ft. Two squadrons took 18 minutes. Three squadrons, about 26 minutes. Four squadrons, 34 to 36 minutes. And five squadrons, which is what Leigh-Mallory was aiming for, took 45 to 48 minutes to form up and get to 20,000ft. By then, the raid it would have been sent to meet would have been over and by using so many squadrons, subsequent raids coming in would arrive unchallenged. The result would have been catastrophe.

'No 12 Group was supposed to cover Biggin Hill, Kenley, Northolt and the other No 11 Group airfields while No 11 Group squadrons were off the ground meeting the Hun coming in. It failed to do this. I know of at least one occasion when Keith Park rang up No 12 Group and said, "You're supposed to be looking after my airfields". He got no change out of that. Of 32 Big Wings sent off by No 12 Group, only seven met the enemy and only once did the Big Wings get there first, before the bombs were dropped.'

Those pilots flying in the Big Wings held the opposite opinion, however. 'There was a feeling among us in No 12 Group that No 11 Group was trying to keep the battle to itself', recalled Sgt David Cox of Fowlmere-based No 19 Squadron. 'We wanted to see more of the action. It was ridiculous if you knew the enemy was a few miles south of you and you weren't supposed to intercept or pursue them. We often didn't take any notice. We went south of the Thames anyway, and it caused a row.

'As for talk that No 12 Group didn't provide cover for No 11 Group when it was asked to, it wasn't as simple as that. Sometimes there was faulty information. Sometimes, when we were asked to cover an airfield and we spotted an enemy not far away, we went after them. It may have been a diversion to get us away. There were mistakes. Once Debden airfield was bombed from 1,000ft, below cloud, while we were sitting up at 15,000ft. That was a mistake, but not ours. The Observer Corps reported the Germans were coming in at 1,000ft, but the No 11 Group controllers just didn't believe it because it had never happened before and they thought a nought had been accidentally left off the report coming in. So the report they passed to us was German bombers at 10,000ft instead of 1,000ft. We were waiting up there, above the cloud. The Germans came in below and we didn't see them. We got the blame. That was unfair.'

Ace Flt Lt Gordon Sinclair served as a flight commander with Czech-manned No 310 Squadron from Duxford, home of the Bader Big Wing:

'We felt the Big Wing was the correct way of operating because you were able to give yourself cover – for example, up sun. If you were flying blind as a single squadron or flight or section and had no cover up sun, you were terribly vulnerable. Flying as a wing, you could move people out to protect your tail, which is what we did.

'We were generally late when called into No 11 Group, but we were operating from 80 miles north of London, while the bombs were being dropped mostly around the Thames Estuary and on the airfields. There was no hope of our getting there if we were alerted late, had delays on the airfield and then had to get to 20,000ft, which took a very long time. Even if the squadrons had gone off in flights, there still would have been those ridiculous delays when we were waiting for clearance to get off the ground. We'd be all ready to take off, pointing into the wind, ready for the word to go. But we had to wait. Our engines would get overheated and out tempers would get frayed. I think it was because of hesitation between the two Group headquarters, saying do we want them off or don't we want them off. There were terrible differences of opinion about who should be called in and when.

'And when we did get off and got down to North Weald, we'd circle there for ages, knowing there was a bloody great battle going on further south. We certainly had the impression that, for reasons we couldn't understand, we weren't called in quickly enough.'

The Big Wing controversy was, however, little more than a distraction at this critical stage in the campaign. The unavoidable facts were that in the final week of August until 2 September, Fighter Command had sustained its heaviest losses, but production of Spitfires and Hurricanes had continued apace and Dowding's reorganisation of his squadrons (including the introduction of foreign-manned units) had ensured that there were enough pilots to man them.

Conversely, the Luftwaffe, for all its recent success, was now starting to struggle in the face of on-going high attrition. For example, it had started the Battle of Britain with more than 900 fighter pilots, but that number had dropped to 735 by 1 September. In the same period the number of operational fighter pilots in the RAF had increased by almost the same margin, although many of these pilots were of course inadequately trained. The Luftwaffe was also struggling to replace aircraft that had been lost, the German aviation industry delivering just 775 Bf 109s between June and September 1940, compared to 1,900 fighters built in Britain that summer. The Jagdwaffe would be particularly stretched in the final phase of the campaign once Kesselring was forced to insist that more than three-quarters of any raiding party had to consist of fighters so as to counter the heavy losses that had so far been sustained by the bombers.

In late August Reichsmarschall Göring went further still, ordering all Jagdgeschwader to remain close to the bombers that they were escorting, and on no account were they to engage enemy fighters unless they or their bombers came under a direct threat of attack. As losses to both German fighters and bombers had mounted, and Fighter Command's resolve seemingly remained intact, senior officers in the Luftwaffe had sought to lay the blame at the feet of the Jagdgeschwader. With the bombers cruising at a much slower speed than the fighters, the Jagdflieger now had to weave in order to maintain station, and yet still retain a high cruising speed in the combat area. By ordering the Jagdwaffe to fly close-formation missions, Göring totally nullified the effectiveness of the previously superior German fighter tactics, thus surrendering the initiative in the skies over southern England.

'We had the impression that, whatever we did, we were bound to be wrong', Major Adolf Galland, Geschwaderkommodore of JG 26, explained. 'Fighter protection for bombers created many problems that

had to be solved in action. Bomber pilots preferred close screening in which their formation was surrounded by pairs of fighters pursuing a zigzag course. Obviously, the visible presence of the protective fighters gave the bomber pilots a greater sense of security. However, this was a faulty conclusion, because a fighter can only carry out this purely defensive task by taking the initiative in the offensive. He must never wait until attacked because he then loses the chance of acting.

'We fighter pilots certainly preferred the free chase during the approach and over the target area. This in fact gave the greatest relief and the best protection for the bomber force, although not perhaps a sense of security for the latter.'

On 3 September Göring had held a conference with all of his senior commanders in The Hague, where he told them that Hitler had had to postpone the invasion to 21 September because the Luftwaffe had not yet been able to subdue the resistance being put up by the RAF. Kesselring remained optimistic that Fighter Command was suffering unsustainable losses and was now drastically short of fighters. He was concerned, however, that the RAF would simply retreat to airfields north of London that were beyond the range of German fighters. Ignorant of the success that his Luftflotten had had against a number of key sector stations since 24 August, and the risk their destruction posed to Fighter Command's defensive system, Kesselring wanted to force the RAF into the air in large numbers so that his more numerous fighter pilots could, finally, shoot them down in large enough numbers to deliver a killer blow to the British. Both he and Göring were of the opinion that only one target could inspire such defence – London.

Sperrle, however, disagreed, being deeply sceptical of the loss reports that both Kesselring and Göring seemed more than happy to accept. He wanted to continue targeting Fighter Command's infrastructure and aircraft factories to prove that the British were in fact far from beaten. With the Führer now calling into question the Luftwaffe's ability to defeat the RAF in time for an invasion, Göring had little choice but to target the capital. Having lost sight of strategic priorities, which would in turn allow the fighter airfields to be repaired and the aircraft factories to resume full production, Göring ordered his Luftflotte to target London. This would prove to be one of the greatest blunders of the Battle of Britain.

Surrounded by his captors, a German airman enjoys a bottle of water and a cigarette prior to being led away into captivity. He was one of 967 Luftwaffe personnel captured during the Battle of Britain.

An effective weapon of war in its day, the He III should have been replaced by faster, heavier four-engined bombers by mid-1940. Nevertheless, it carried a heavier bombload than any of its contemporaries then in frontline service with the Luftwaffe.

This Dornier Do 17Z of 9./KG 76 was attacking RAF Biggin Hill on 18 August, when it was shot down by Hurricanes of No 111 Squadron and crashed at Leaves Green, Kent.

Sgt Joan Mortimer, Cpl Elspeth Candlish-Henderson and Sgt Helen Turner each received the Military Medal
for remaining at their posts when Biggin Hill came under heavy aerial bombardment in August 1940.

Major Oesau
Träger des Eichenlaubs mit Schwertern
zum Ritterkreuz des Eisernen Kreuzes

R 187

WALTER OESAU

Hauptmann

Originally joining the Wehrmacht as an enlisted soldier in 1933 and serving in the Second Artillery Regiment, Walter 'Gulle' Oesau was transferred to a Luftwaffe transport unit the following year. He was assigned to JG 132 in 1936 and saw combat with 3./J 88 (led by Werner Mölders) in Spain in 1938, claiming eight victories during 130 missions. In March 1939 Oesau joined I./JG 2 and three months later he was made Staffelkapitän of 2./JG 20. He claimed six victories with this unit during the Battle of France and on the eve of the Battle of Britain I./JG 20 became III./JG 51. Oesau would enjoy considerable success during the summer and autumn of 1940, taking his tally to 47 victories by 1 November – he had also been awarded the Knight's Cross. Subsequently serving in command positions with JGs 3, 2 and 1, he was eventually shot down and killed in combat over Belgium on 11 May 1944. By then he had claimed 127 victories, 74 of them in the West.

'Walter 'Gulle' Oesau was the toughest fighter pilot in the Luftwaffe'

JOHANNES 'MACKI' STEINHOFF

On 19 July III./JG 51 confronted Defiants of No 141 Squadron south of Folkestone. Oesau and his pilots soon gained the advantage and claimed 11 Defiants.

Major Adolf Galland's Bf 109-equipped JG 26 brought the Defiant's brief, but bloody, career as a day-fighter to an end on 28 August when it claimed three of the type destroyed. No 264 Squadron was attempting to intercept 20 He 111s near Folkestone. Galland was credited with the demise of one of the Defiants for his 23rd victory.

A ground line-up of No 264 Squadron Defiants. Tragically this unit would go on to lose nine aircraft and 14 aircrew in just three engagements on 24, 26 and 28 August, resulting in the type's permanent removal from No 11 Group as a day-fighter.

No 264 Squadron led by Sqn Ldr Philip Hunter in N1535/PS-A. Hunter was ultimately lost in this machine whilst chasing a Ju 88 over the Channel on 24 August. Behind N1535 is L7026/PS-V, which Plt Off Eric Barwell used to shoot down a Bf 109 on the same day.

A No 64 Squadron pilot races towards his Spitfire at RAF Kenley in mid August – note his parachute on the tailplane of the fighter.

British 'Tommies' carry away the starboard fin from Bf 110C Wk-Nr 3113 of 3./ZG 2, which was shot down by three Hurricanes from No 17 Squadron on 3 September 1940. The crew bailed out before the Zerstörer crashed at Pudsey Hill Farm, Essex.

Having consulted his map, this He 111 observer confers with his pilot over an impending direction change en route to a target on 15 August 1940.

ALL MY OWN WORK BY GRIMES   With acknowledgments To "THE STAR"

"These two German airmen want you to give them
a lift to the police station."
"O.K.   But tell 'em they ride at their own risk."

Priller's dry sense of humour extended to combat. When one of his junior pilots got separated over England and cried out for help over the radio reporting that he was alone over London, Priller, who could see the pilot clearly, told him not to worry because two Spitfires were closing with him from behind and he would not be alone for much longer.

JOSEF 'PIPS' PRILLER

Oberleutnant

Known throughout his military career as 'Pips', Josef Priller claimed 100 victories in total, all in the West. Joining the Wehrmacht in 1935, he switched to the Luftwaffe the following year and initially served with I./JG 135. By September 1939 the unit had become II./JG 51, and the following month Priller was made Staffelkapitän of the Gruppe's 6. Staffel. Leading 6./JG 51 throughout the Battles of France and Britain, Priller had claimed 20 victories and been awarded the Knight's Cross (he later received the Oak Leaves and Swords as well) by the time he was transferred to I./JG 26 as Staffelkapitän in late November 1940. Promoted to Gruppenkommandeur of III./JG 26 in December 1941, Priller became Kommodore of the Jagdgeschwader in January 1943. He would remain in this position until made Inspekteur der Jagdflieger West on 31 January 1945, thus bringing his operational flying to an end. A veteran of 1,307 sorties, Priller's victories included at least 68 Spitfires and 11 four-engined bombers.

Oberleutnant 'Pips' Priller of 6./JG 51 crosses the French coastline in his Bf 109E during the Battle of Britain.

JAMES NICOLSON VC

Flight Commander

James Nicolson joined the RAF in 1936 and was assigned to No 249 Squadron as a flight commander in May 1940. On 16 August he was shot down after being bounced by Bf 110s over Southampton. Wounded in the left foot and with a perspex splinter through his left eyelid, Nicolson was about to abandon his burning Hurricane when a Bf 110 appeared in front of him. Sliding back into the cockpit, he fired at the Zerstörer until he could stand the flames no longer. Nicolson baled out at 12,000ft, suffering from severe burns to his hands and parts of his face, a partially severed eyelid and a badly wounded foot. He was also shot in the buttock by Local Defence Volunteers as he neared the ground. For this action, Nicolson was awarded Fighter Command's only VC of the battle. Sadly Nicolson was killed on 2 May 1945 when a Liberator that he was onboard suffered an engine fire during a bombing mission and crashed into the Bay of Bengal.

During the afternoon of 28 August 1940, Prime Minister Winston Churchill was touring the defences in and around Dover Castle when he witnessed an engagement between a Bf 109E from 2./JG 3 and a Spitfire from No 610 Squadron. The engine of the Messerschmitt, flown by Leutnant Herbert Landry, burst into flames and the pilot baled out with serious wounds – he subsequently died on 23 September. Churchill visited the crash site a short while later, picking up a cartridge case as a souvenir. The shattered remains of the still-smouldering Bf 109 can just be seen.

Landry's victor was Yorkshireman Sgt Ronnie Hamlyn of No 610 Squadron, who, four days earlier, had achieved the rare accolade of 'ace-in-a-day' when he claimed four Bf 109Es and a Ju 88 destroyed.

Spitfires of No 610 'County of Chester' Squadron head out for a Channel patrol from Gravesend in early June 1940. The unit had seen much action over France during Operation 'Dynamo' and lessons learned during this period are reflected in the loose line-astern formations flown by two of the three sections.

ERIC LOCK

Pilot Officer

Nicknamed 'Sawn Off Lockie' because of his extremely short stature, Eric Lock had joined the RAF Volunteer Reserve in 1939 and was called-up in September 1939. He completed his training in the early summer of 1940 and was posted to No 41 Squadron at Catterick. He claimed his first success during Luftflotte 5's fateful mission on 15 August when he downed a Bf 110. Lock's unit was then posted south to Hornchurch on 3 September and by the end of the month his score stood at 17 victories. Receiving a DFC for this success on 1 October, Lock had increased his tally to 23 kills by 17 November. However, shortly after claiming two Bf 109s destroyed on this mission he was jumped by a third fighter from JG 54 and badly wounded, crash-landing at RAF Martlesham Heath. Lock would spend the next six months recovering in hospital. Posted to No 611 Squadron as a flight commander in July 1941, he had taken his score to 26 victories by the time he was lost on 3 August after strafing German soldiers on a road near Calais.

Plt Off Ludwik Martel (above) was a Polish pilot who saw considerable action in the Battle of Britain with both Nos 54 and 603 Squadrons, claiming a Bf 109 destroyed with the latter unit on 5 October. Martel was wounded in action on 25 October 1940 whilst at the controls of Spitfire IIA P7350. This aircraft remains in service with the RAF Battle of Britain Memorial Flight and is seen in the colours of Eric Lock's No 41 Squadron Spitfire IA N3162/EB-G. Also featured is the Flight's Hurricane IIC LF363 wearing the colours of No 1 Squadron P3395/JX-B, which was the personal mount of ace Sgt Arthur 'Darkie' Clowes during the battle.

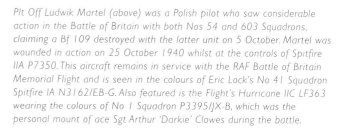

No 41 Squadron Spitfires head out on patrol from Hornchurch in September 1940. The unit claimed 91.333 victories during the Battle of Britain, with 34 of these being Bf 109Es. One of the highest scoring squadrons of the campaign, it was engaged for 30 days during the summer and autumn of 1940, losing 27 Spitfires in combat. One of those aircraft was X4178/EB-K, seen here leading the formation. It was shot down by Oberleutnant Josef Fözö of 4./JG 51 (his 13th victory, which he actually claimed as a Hurricane), during the morning of 15 October, the fighter crashing into the Channel. Its pilot, 23-year-old Sgt Philip Lloyd, was killed.

Oberst Galland
Träger des Eichenlaubs zum Ritterkreuz des Eisernen Kreuzes

Luftwaffe JG26 Photo Diary

This remarkable series of photographs was taken during 1939-40 by Oberleutnant Rolf Schrödter, the Technical Officer of III./JG 26. They offer a rare glimpse into the life of a frontline Jagdgeschwader during the first 16 months of World War 2. Some of the famous faces seen in this selection of photographs include Oberstleutnant Adolf Galland, Hauptmann Rolf Pingel, Hauptmann 'Gerd' Schöpfel, Oberleutnant Gustav 'Micky' Sprick, Oberleutnant Joachim Müncheberg, Major Werner Mölders and the Führer himself.

On a rare visit to a frontline unit, the Führer joined JG 26 at Château Bonnance, near its airfield at Abbeville, for Christmas dinner. Accompanied throughout his brief stay by Geschwaderkommodore Oberstleutnant Adolf Galland, Hitler was flanked by Hauptmann Rolf Pingel and Hauptmann 'Gerd' Schöpfel during his festive meal.

Bf 109E-1 'Yellow 11' was written off in a forced landing by Feldwebel Artur Beese of 9./JG 26 after his fighter had been shot up by Sgt Ronnie Hamlyn of No 610 Squadron on 24 August – one of five victories claimed by the RAF ace on this date. III./JG 26 and two other Gruppen sortied 66 Bf 109Es in total as escorts for 40 Ju 88s and Do 17s targeting Dover in an early morning mission, and three of its Bf 109s were lost that day. Beese just managed to coax his bullet-riddled fighter back over the French coast, coming down in the sand dunes near St Inglevert. Whilst this aircraft was written-off, many were salvaged and repaired to fly again, often by groundcrew working in open air conditions.

All 9./JG 26 aircraft carried the red Hollenhund Staffel emblem on both sides of the fuselage beneath the cockpit in the summer of 1940, as well as the Geschwader 'Schlageter' shield. Here 'Yellow 9' is being inspected after a forced landing.

A Bf 109E-4 of 7./JG 26 has its engine serviced between sorties in early August 1940. Oberleutnant Joachim Müncheberg was made Staffelkäpitan of 7./JG 26 later that month.

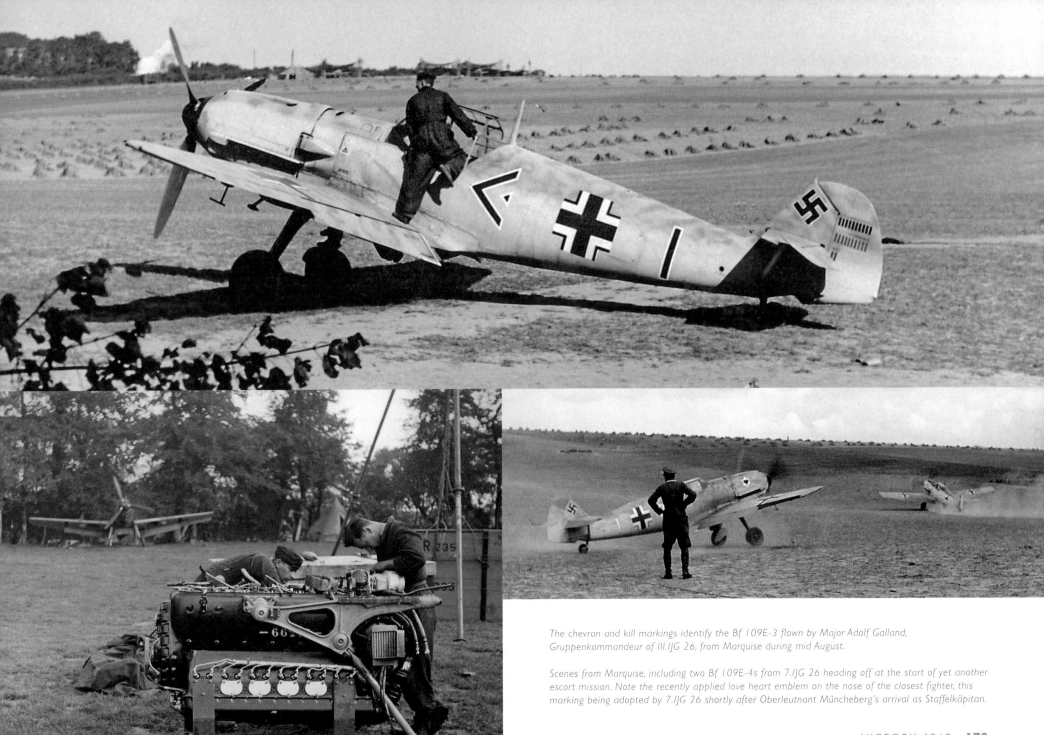

The chevron and kill markings identify the Bf 109E-3 flown by Major Adolf Galland, Gruppenkommandeur of III./JG 26, from Marquise during mid August.

Scenes from Marquise, including two Bf 109E-4s from 7./JG 26 heading off at the start of yet another escort mission. Note the recently applied love heart emblem on the nose of the closest fighter, this marking being adopted by 7./JG 26 shortly after Oberleutnant Müncheberg's arrival as Staffelkäpitan.

ADOLF MALAN

Nicknamed 'Sailor' following an early career in the South African merchant navy, Malan joined the RAF on a short service commission in late 1935. Posted to No 74 Squadron in December of the following year, he was a veteran flight commander by the time World War 2 commenced. Having 'made ace' over Dunkirk, Malan was an early recipient of the DFC in June 1940. He became CO of No 74 Squadron on 8 August and he wrote his seminal 'Ten Rules of Air Fighting' shortly thereafter – this was widely distributed throughout Fighter Command. By the time Malan left No 74 Squadron in March 1941 to head up the Biggin Hill Wing, he had claimed 15 victories and been awarded a DSO. He was credited with 12 more kills (all Bf109s) up to 24 July 1941, when he was posted out of the frontline. Malan spent the rest of the war in staff positions, being station commander at Biggin Hill for 10 months in 1943 – he routinely flew on operations during this time, but scored no more victories. Ending the war with the rank of group captain, Malan returned with his family to South Africa in 1946.

GEORGE UNWIN

Joining the RAF as an apprentice clerk in 1929, George Unwin eventually applied for pilot training and commenced his wings course in November 1935. He joined No 19 Squadron at Duxford the following year, and gained vast experience on the Spitfire when the unit became the first in Fighter Command to receive the aeroplane in August 1938. Claiming early victories with the aircraft over Dunkirk, Unwin continued to build up his tally during the Battle of Britain while flying primarily as part of No 12 Group's controversial Big Wing. Awarded a DFM on 1 October, Unwin's tally stood at 13 and two shared destroyed, two unconfirmed destroyed, two probables and one damaged by the time he left No 19 Squadron for Training Command in December 1940. Despite being the unit's ranking ace, Fighter Command had deemed Unwin too old (he was almost 28!) for further frontline flying. He eventually returned to operations in April 1944 when he joined No 613 Squadron, equipped with Mosquitos. Unwin led Brigand-equipped No 84 Squadron in combat over Malaya in 1950-51, receiving a DSO for his service.

ALAN DEERE

Kiwi Al Deere had applied to join the RAF on a short service commission in New Zealand and he commenced his flying training in November 1937. Ten months later he was posted to No 54 Squadron, which began to receive Spitfires from March 1939. Deere emerged from the action over France in late May 1940 with seven and one shared victories to his credit, although he was himself shot down on 28 May – he returned to No 54 Squadron after an epic 19-hour journey from Dunkirk. Deere was presented with a DFC by the King on 27 June. Deere was lucky to survive the Battle of Britain. He was shot down twice (once by a Spitfire), had to force land once and his Spitfire was also blown up on take-off during an air-raid on Hornchurch. Following a well-earned period of rest, he joined No 602 Squadron and subsequently commanded this unit and No 403 Squadron. Made Wing Leader at Biggin Hill in the spring of 1943, he claimed his final victory on 23 June that year – by which time his score stood at 17 and one shared destroyed. He remained in the RAF post-war, eventually retiring with the rank of air commodore in 1967.

WILLIAM MILLINGTON

Born in England and having grown up in Australia, Bill Millington joined the RAF on a short service commission in June 1939. Upon completing his 16-day conversion to Hurricanes, he joined No 79 Squadron at Biggin Hill on 17 June 1940. Despite his lack of experience in the fighter, Millington claimed eight victories in just a few weeks, including three He 111s on 15 August and two Bf 109s and a Do 17 on 31 August. His Hurricane was set alight during the latter combat, however, and although having suffered a thigh wound and burns, he stayed with the fighter and force-landed near Hawkhurst, in Kent – Millington feared the aeroplane might crash into the village if he abandoned it. Upon recovery, he was posted to No 249 Squadron at North Weald on 19 September. Awarded a DFC on 1 October, Millington made a further seven claims prior to being posted missing after he failed to return from a clash with German fighters over the Channel on 30 October. His final tally was nine and two shared destroyed, four probables and three damaged.

JOHANNES TRAUTLOFT

Kommodore of JG 54 during the latter stages of the Battle of Britain, Hannes Trautloft received his military training with the 'secret Luftwaffe' in the USSR in 1932. Sent to gain combat experience in Spain in August 1936, he claimed the Condor Legion's first aerial victory. Five days later Trautloft became the first German pilot to be shot down during the conflict. Credited with five victories in Spain, and helping to develop effective combat tactics for the Bf 109, Trautloft eventually returned home and served with various fighter units in leading up to World War 2. A veteran of combat in Poland with 2./JG 77 and in France with I./JG 20 (which became III./JG 51 in July 1940), Trautloft was given command of JG 54 the following month. He led the Jagdgeschwader until made an Inspector of Fighters in July 1943. By then he had claimed 58 victories (including seven RAF fighters in 1940) during 560 sorties. Highly regarded by his contemporaries, Trautloft survived the war and eventually reached the rank of generalleutnant in the Bundeswehr.

ADOLF GALLAND

Arguably Germany's most famous fighter ace of World War 2, Galland joined the Luftwaffe in 1934. A veteran of combat in Spain, where he saw plenty of action in the ground-support role rather than as a fighter pilot, Galland eventually succeeded in being posted to Bf 109E-equipped JG 27 in April 1940. He claimed his first success on 12 May when he downed an RAF Hurricane, and by the end of the Battle of France Galland's tally stood at 12. Transferred to JG 26 as Gruppenkomandeur of III. Gruppe shortly before the Battle of Britain, he famously led from the front. Galland received the Knight's Cross on 1 August after claiming his 17th success and was promoted to Geschwaderkommodore of JG 26 three weeks later. He received Oak Leaves for his Knight's Cross on 25 September (and, subsequently, the Swords and Diamonds), by which time his victory tally stood at 40, and he claimed his 50th kill on 1 November. Made General der Jagdflieger a year later, Adolf Galland ultimately survived the war with 100 victories to his name – the last six came in April 1945 whilst flying the Me 262 with JV 44.

HERBERT IHLEFELD

Herbert Ihlefeld was credited with more Spitfire I/IIs destroyed than any other Luftwaffe pilot. Joining the Luftwaffe in 1933, he claimed nine victories flying Bf 109Bs in Spain with 2./J 88 in 1938-39. Ihlefeld was serving with I.(J)/LG 2 when Germany invaded Poland and he saw combat here and during the Battle of France. He claimed the first of 33 Spitfire I/IIs credited to him on 30 June. Made Gruppenkommandeur of I.(J)/LG 2 on 30 August, Ihlefeld downed no fewer than 15 Spitfires in September alone, being awarded the Knight's Cross that same month. He led the unit in action both in Yugoslavia and on the Eastern Front in 1941. Scoring heavily in the latter theatre, Ihlefeld became only the fifth pilot in the Jagdwaffe to reach the 100-kill mark on 22 April 1942. Subsequently leading JGs 52, 103, 25, 11 and 1, he scored his final 13 victories during Defence of the Reich operations in 1944. He was also awarded the Oak Leaves and Swords to his Knight's Cross. Ihlefeld survived the war with 122 victories to his name, having flown more than 1,000 combat missions.

JOACHIM MÜNCHEBERG

Germany's fifth ranking ace in the West, Joachim Müncheberg joined the Luftwaffe from the Wehrmacht in 1938. Claiming his first 13 victories as Gruppenadjutant of III./JG 26, he became Staffelkapitän of 7./JG 26 on 21 August 1940. Awarded the Knight's Cross the following month (to which he later added the Oak Leaves and Swords), Müncheberg's tally stood at 23 kills when he and his Staffel were detached to Sicily in early 1941. Enjoying incredible success over Malta, his score stood at 48 when Müncheberg returned to the Channel front. He became Gruppenkommandeur of II./JG 26 in September 1941 and Kommodore of JG 51 on the Eastern Front in July 1942. Müncheberg achieved his 100th victory on 5 September 1942 and was transferred to North Africa to take charge of JG 77 shortly thereafter. On 23 March 1943, while flying his 500th sortie, Müncheberg attacked an American Spitfire whose pilot, Capt Theodore Sweetland, reportedly collided with him. Both men were killed. By the time of his death, Müncheberg's victory tally stood at 134, with 102 kills claimed in the West.

WERNER MÖLDERS

The leading German ace of the Spanish Civil War, Werner Mölders was instrumental in the development of the new fighter tactics so effectively employed by the Luftwaffe in World War 2. He had joined the Luftwaffe in 1934 and duly served with several units prior to commanding Bf 109B-equipped 3./J 88 in Spain in 1938. Joining JG 53 upon his return to Germany, Mölders had taken his tally to 38 victories (and received the Knight's Cross) by the time he was himself shot down and captured during the Battle of France on 5 June 1940. Released after the French capitulation, he was posted to JG 51 as its Kommodore the following month and remained in the vanguard of the action with the Geschwader during the Battle of Britain. In 1941 JG 51 was transferred east in preparation for the invasion of the USSR, where, between 22 June and 15 July, Mölders took his final tally to 108 victories. Removed from the frontline and made the Inspector General of Fighters, he was killed in a flying accident on 22 November 1941 travelling to the funeral of his superior officer, World War 1 ace Generaloberst Ernst Udet.

PHASE THREE
The Blitz

· ·

"If you **Wrong Us**
shall **We** not
Revenge?"

The Merchant of Venice, Act III, Scene I

William Shakespeare

With the iconic Tower Bridge in the foreground, a westerly breeze pushes smoke from blazing dockside warehouses across the East End of London during the evening of 7 September. This photograph by Albert E. Creffield of the New York Times was taken while the raid was still in progress.

Taken at 18.48hrs German time on 7 September 1940, an He 111H flies over Wapping and the characteristic U-bend of the Thames that was designated by the Luftwaffe as Zielräum (Target Area) G – the area inside the U-bend. There were three Target Areas in London, within which lay a variable number of key sites that had been identified for bombing. Zielräum A encompassed the Elephant and Castle to Blackfriars Bridge district and part of the East End, while Zielräum E covered north of the Thames, as well as parts of west and northwest London. Note the shadow cast by Tower Bridge in the top left-hand corner.

The Blitz, which commenced on the afternoon of 7 September, was a sustained strategic bombing campaign against Great Britain and Northern Ireland by the Luftwaffe. Continuing until 16 May 1941, it saw London attacked 71 times, Birmingham, Liverpool and Plymouth eight times, Bristol six, Glasgow five, Southampton four and Portsmouth three.

The "whitest" man I know!

London was bombed for 57 consecutive nights, with more than one million houses destroyed or damaged. In excess of 40,000 civilians were killed during the Blitz, almost half of those in London. Aside from bombing the docks in the East End, the commercial areas of west London were also hit, as were St Paul's Cathedral and Buckingham Palace – the latter two by mistake, as the Führer had forbidden Luftwaffe crews from deliberately targeting sites of cultural importance.

London's Burning

Up until the devastating raid on London on the afternoon of 7 September 1940, both the Luftwaffe and the RAF had carefully avoided wholesale attacks on major cities in an effort to escape the cycle of destruction that had been predicted by politicians and military strategists alike throughout the 1930s. Indeed, Hitler had expressly forbidden the Luftwaffe from attacking targets in London without first gaining his permission. As early as 15 August, however, German Bf 110 fighter-bombers had accidentally hit factories surrounding Croydon airport (they were meant to be attacking Kenley airfield), on the southwestern outskirts of London. Little damage was done and the British government chose to ignore it.

On the night of 24/25 August a force of 100 He 111s had attempted to bomb the oil terminal at Thameshaven, in southeast London. Hitting a precise target such as this in the dark skies over the blacked-out suburbs of the capital was always going to be hard and the bombers missed the oil terminal and struck the residential quarter of the East End instead. In retaliation, the British government approved raids by Bomber Command on Berlin – the first such mission was flown on 28/29 August. The damage done to the city was not extensive, but the damage done to the pride of the Nazi leadership was enormous. They were furious and vowed that the British would pay dearly for their impudence. Hitler immediately lifted his veto on targeting London.

The opening raid on the capital was mounted during the afternoon of 7 September. Code-named Operation 'Loge' (God of Fire), this phase of the campaign would be overseen by Göring himself – although Kesselring and his staff had in fact done all the planning for attacks on London prior to the Battle of Britain actually commencing. The Reichsmarschall, having been goaded into personal action by his frustration at the lack of identifiable progress in the destruction of Fighter Command, arrived in the Pas-de-Calais on his personal train on the eve of the operation.

Shortly before 16.00hrs on the 7th the first 'hostile' raid was picked by coastal radar operators and plotted. Within minutes the radar screens had lit up as wave after wave of German aeroplanes crossed the Channel. Almost 350 bombers from five Kampfgeschwader, accompanied by 617 Bf 109s and Bf 110s – virtually every serviceable aircraft that Luftflotten 2 and 3 could muster – headed for London in gathering formations that were two miles high, staggered between 14,000ft and 23,000ft.

'The assembly of the bombers and fighters took place in the vicinity of our fighter bases over some landmark on the coast at a predetermined altitude and zero hour', recalled Major Adolf Galland, 'It happened more than once that the bombers arrived late. As a result, the fighters joined another bomber formation which had already met its fighter escort and thus flew doubly protected, while the belated formation had either to turn back or make an unescorted raid usually resulting in heavy losses. Radio or radar guidance for such an assembly was not available – even our intercom did not work most of the time.

'All formations had to take the shortest route to London because the escorting fighters had a reserve of only 10min combat time. Large-scale decoy manoeuvres or circumnavigation of the British AA zone were therefore impossible. The anti-aircraft barrage around London was of considerable strength and concentration and seriously hampered the target approach of the bombers. The balloon barrage over and around the capital made low-level attacks and dive-bombing impossible. The bulk of the English fighters were sent up to encounter the German raiders just before they reached their target. I know of no instance in which they managed to prevent the bombers reaching their target, but they inflicted heavy losses both on them and the German escort fighters.'

Within 30 minutes of the formations' detection every squadron within a 70-mile radius of the capital (21 in total) was either airborne or at readiness. To Dowding and Park it seemed clear that the Luftwaffe was heading for the battered sector airfields yet again. However, instead of splitting up, the formations, covering 800 square miles of sky, advanced towards London. By the time No 11 Group had realised this and vectored fighters towards Thames Haven and Tilbury, the first bombs were already dropping on the docks and the East End.

'I'd never seen so many aircraft', explained No 602 Squadron CO, Sqn Ldr Sandy Johnstone. It was a hazy sort of day right up to about 16,000ft. As we broke through the haze you could hardly believe it. As far as you could see, there was nothing but German aircraft coming in, wave after wave, all heading for London. I have never seen so many aircraft in the air all at the same time. The escorting fighters saw us at once and came down on us like a ton of bricks, then the squadron split up and the sky became a seething cauldron of aeroplanes, swooping and swerving in and out of the vapour trails and tracer smoke. A Hurricane on fire spun out of control ahead of me while, above to my right, a 110 flashed across my vision and disappeared into the fog of battle before I could draw a bead on it. Everyone was shouting at once and the earphones became filled with a meaningless cacophony of jumbled noises. Everything became a maelstrom of jumbled impression – a Dornier spinning wildly with part of its port mainplane missing; black streaks of tracer ahead, when I instinctively put my arm up to shield my face; taking a breather when the haze absorbed me for a moment.'

The Kampfgeschwader dropped their ordnance mainly on the docks and factories that lined the Thames, although some bombs fell as far west as Kensington. Once the late-arriving units of No 11 Group arrived on the scene, the German armada had turned for home. The Spitfire and Hurricane units quickly set about shooting down 41 aircraft, more than half of them fighters. The RAF lost 22 aeroplanes and had 10 pilots killed – no fewer than 448 civilians were also killed. Flying Hurricanes from Northolt, to the west of London, No 303 'Polish' Squadron found itself in the thick of the action. Amongst the pilots to enjoy success that day was future ace Plt Off Jan Zumbach, who claimed two Do 17s destroyed:

'We were climbing at full speed when I saw a burst of ack-ack fire over London harbour and then, a little to the right, below us, a formation of German bombers escorted by a surprisingly large number of Me 109s. Coming from the south, the bombers approached the Thames to drop their bombs and then turn north. I thought we were going to rush at the enemy, but this was not so. It seemed that our squadron leader, a British officer, did not realise exactly which direction the bombers were taking. Then I heard someone shout in Polish, "Attack! Follow me!" It was Plt Off Paszkiewicz, a very experienced pilot, who shook his wings to show the others he was leaving the formation. He started to attack and was immediately followed by the other sections, and also by out leader, who now understood the manoeuvre.

'In front of me, two Dorniers were already on fire and parachutes were opening in the sky. The German bombers were approaching at tremendous speed. My leader was already firing. It was my turn. I pressed the button. Nothing happened. I swore violently. Already I had

to move out. Tracer bullets were whizzing by on all sides and then I realised I had forgotten to release the safety catch.

'Turning violently, crushed down by centrifugal force, bent in two, I found myself on the tail of a stream of bombers, with a Do 17 in front of me growing bigger and bigger in my sights, until it blotted out everything else. I saw the rear gunner aiming at me. I pressed the button and the rattle of eight machine guns shook my aeroplane. A long cloud of smoke came out of the Dornier's left engine. Another burst and it was ablaze. Over the radio, everyone was shouting, in English, in Polish.

'I saw a Hurricane having trouble with a bandit. I was about to rush to his help when the Hurricane burst into flames. A parachute opened up almost immediately. It was Plt Off Daszewski who had been able to bale out after losing half of his left buttock to a burst of Messerschmitt gunfire. Flg Off Pisarek also had to jump, leaving one of his boots stuck in his burning aeroplane. He landed in a suburban garden full of roses. A man came over to help him and said, "Sir, I would like you to know this is private property", and then invited him to tea. Pisarek was terribly embarrassed because he was without that missing boot and he had a hole in his sock.'

That evening more bombers targeted London to signal the start of the night Blitz, 318 aircraft attacking from 20.10hrs through to 04.30hrs the following morning. The capital would be targeted every night for the next 57 days. 'It was burning all down the river', Air Vice-Marshal Park noted in his diary on 8 September, 'but I looked down and said "Thank God for that", because I knew that the Nazis had switched their attacks from the fighter stations thinking they were knocked out. They weren't, but they were pretty groggy'.

With London now being attacked both during the day and at night, the RAF had to hastily find a way to take the fight to the enemy after dark. During the war the primary defence against night bombers was the radar-equipped nightfighter. During the Battle of Britain, the RAF had only a handful of ex-day fighter Blenheim IFs flying with experimental Air Interception radar, which were proving to be unreliable. Despite its modest record at night, the Blenheim IF was used by a handful of pilots to achieve aerial victories. One of the most successful was New Zealander, and future ace, Plt Off Mike Herrick of No 25 Squadron, based at North Weald. He destroyed two He 111s in a single mission over Essex on 4/5 September, stating in his combat report that 'the

A failed attempt to bomb the oil terminal at Thameshaven proved to be the catalyst for the start of the the Blitz, thereby changing the course of the war. The Luftwaffe successfully hit the target on 3 November 1940.

searchlights were most effective and, of course, entirely responsible in enabling me to sight and fire at the enemy'. His squadron mate Plt Off N H 'Paddy' Corry recalled the night:

'Mike suddenly found himself right up the backside of a big fat Heinkel [as a result of guidance from the ground controller] and did everything just about right. Then, on the way home, he nearly collided with a second Heinkel – which fell to pieces after a burst fired at less than 30 yards. I believe it was the first of the two bombers that gave Mike a bad time. During his attack Mike's windscreen was shattered and he had perspex debris in his eyes, which made his second visual contact and attack all the more remarkable.'

Flying alongside the Blenheim IFs and, towards the end of 1940, Beaufighters, were six squadrons of Hurricanes and Defiants (relegated to nightfighter duties after their mauling as day fighters early on in the Battle of Britain), whose only real modification for the task was that they were painted black. In 491 sorties on 46 nights, they shot down 11 German aircraft that pilots located with general guidance from ground controllers in the sector operations rooms and by direct observation in the light of fires or searchlights.

The night raid proved to be critically important for the Luftwaffe, which would struggle to replicate the 7 September daylight raid on a daily basis. There was little Fighter Command could do to oppose them and the Germans knew this. Only a small number of German aircraft were downed during the night Blitz – 54 due to enemy action (mainly flak) and 12 in accidents up to the end of 1940, which was a mere one per cent of the sorties dispatched.

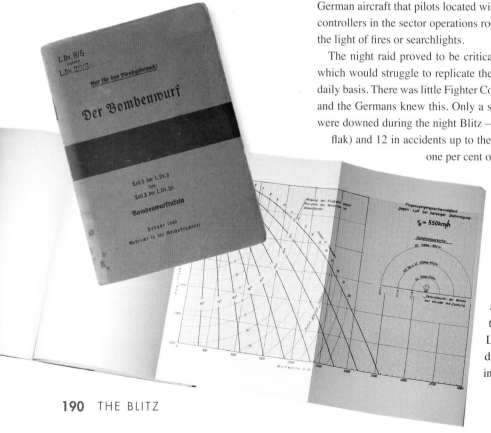

The next large-scale daylight raid occurred on 9 September, and this time Park was prepared. The Luftwaffe approached in a pincer movement consisting of two separate formations, and No 11 Group's fighters were airborne and ready to intercept them well before they reached London. The first formation dropped its bombs on Canterbury instead, while the second was so badly mauled that it scattered and dropped ordnance all over Surrey and Kent. The RAF downed 24 aircraft and, more importantly, had saved London from being bombed. Seventeen of the aircraft lost were Bf 109s and Bf 110s, reflecting their vulnerability now that they had been ordered to stay close to the bombers. Indeed, losses amongst the Bf 109E Geschwader in particular rose steeply once they were 'chained' to the bomber formations and one of those men shot down was six-victory ace Feldwebel Heinrich Hoehnisch of 1./JG 53:

'On my last mission, on 9 September 1940, our task was to give direct fighter cover to the rear of an He 111 bomber formation. One Kette [three aircraft in a "vic" formation] of bombers got separated, so our Staffel looked after them. We had only seven Bf 109s, and I was tail-end Charlie with Oberfeldwebel Mueller.

'Flying in the direction of London docks, there was no contact with the enemy, but I was sure that we could expect attacks out of the sun as soon as we turned 180° for our return flight. To my surprise, I saw, when I was looking towards the rest of my Staffel, six Spitfires on a reciprocal course in line astern about 50 metres above me. To avoid the inevitable attack, I tried to come up with my Staffel flying in front and below me. When I was level with my Staffelkapitän, I thought I had made it. However, there was a rattle like an explosion in my aeroplane and, with the pressure of a blowtorch, flames hit my face. With the greatest difficulty, I got out of my aeroplane. I landed with severe burns to my face and bullet wounds to my right calf. I stayed in the hospital in Woolwich for two months.'

Hoehnisch had been shot down by No 19 Squadron Spitfire ace Flt Lt Wilf Clouston in a brief engagement that had lasted just a matter of seconds – a typical example of the Spitfire-versus-Bf 109E clashes that occurred throughout the Battle of Britain.

A further spate of poor weather gave Air Vice-Marshal Park time to study recent combat reports from his pilots and then issue more specific instructions over the course of the next five days to ensure greater success against the massed formations of bombers that had frequently been engaged during the first two weeks of September. He recommended head-on attacks, as they had proven the most effective since the very start of the Battle of Britain. A veteran of the fighting over Dunkirk with No 65 Squadron, Flt Lt Brian Kingcome had transferred to No 92 Squadron as a flight commander shortly thereafter. Often leading the unit into action, he was an advocate of the head-on attack:

'If you did what had been considered to be the normal thing and came around behind the bombers to bust up their formation, their fighter escorts would get to you before you could get to them. Also, the rear guns of a tightly packed bomber formation could bring a huge concentration of fire to bear on you. But if you attacked them from the front, it was very frightening for the bomber pilot. He saw a fighter coming straight at him. He didn't have protective armour plate. As you came at him, you'd see him nervously getting ready for you, bouncing around long before you were within firing range. If you were a German pilot sitting at the front of a bomber with your rear gunners and a whole lot of metal behind you, when there was an attack from the rear you couldn't really see what was happening back there. So you went droning on towards your target. But if the attack was coming right at you personally, you were in the frontline. You'd see the tracers flashing past and the enemy coming at you. They had to be very, very tough and very, very brave to keep going steadily onward.'

One of the most successful exponents of the head-on attack was Sqn Ldr Gerry Edge, who had flown Hurricanes in France and during the Battle of Britain with No 605 Squadron before becoming the CO No 253 Squadron in early September. He claimed at least 20 victories during 1940, 11 of them between 7 and 15 September:

'If you left it till your last hundred yards to break away from a head-on attack, you were in trouble. With practice, you got to judge when to break. But once you knew how, a head-on attack was a piece of cake. When you opened fire, you'd rake the line of them as you broke away. On one attack, the first Heinkel I hit crashed into the next Heinkel. There was a lot of crashing among the bombers we attacked head-on.'

Plt Off 'Paddy' Barthropp of No 602 Squadron had nothing but respect for such attacks by his contemporaries:

'A few brave buggers used to do head-on attacks. Bloody dangerous. There were one or two lunatics who revelled in it. The chance of hitting something going head-on was pretty remote unless you were attacking a big formation of bombers. Then you'd rake them, getting your nose up and down, knowing something was going to connect. That was very effective.'

Flt Lt Pete Brothers, was one of those 'brave buggers':

'The urgent thing was to get at the bombers before they dropped their bombs, and if you were short of height you wanted to carry out a stern or beam attack. The best thing to do, however, was to take

them head-on and go straight through the formation. I always dived beneath the bombers short of impact because I always thought that the instinctive thing for pilots to do was to pull up rather than push down when faced with collision, and the last thing I wanted was to meet a Dornier or Heinkel at close quarters. This manoeuvre also produced additional speed, thus enabling me to pull the Hurricane around once clear of the bombers and turn back into them for a more concentrated stern attack.

'Head-on shots were the easiest of the lot to perform because there was no deflection needed whatsoever. I would press home the attack until I thought a collision was almost inevitable. In many respects this was the best form of attack, as most bombers had less protection from both guns and armour at the front.'

Heinkel He IIIH of 7./KG I 'Hindenburg' in formation en route to London for another bombing mission.

ACES
in ART

'*Behind the bombers I could see the fighter escort stepped up in layers above their charges, and they couldn't touch us until after we had carried out the first attack on the bombers!*'

BRIAN LANE

BRIAN LANE

Squadron Leader

Brian 'Sandy' Lane chose a career in the RAF after he lost his job as a supervisor in an electric bulb factory, commencing his flying training in March 1936. Joining No 66 Squadron at Duxford in January of the following year, he was posted to No 213 Squadron upon its reformation six months later. Lane was transferred to No 19 Squadron as a flight commander in September 1939, and he took temporary charge of the unit after his CO was killed over Dunkirk on 25 May 1940. He led No 19 Squadron again from 5 September after the death of yet another commanding officer, 'Sandy' Lane claiming six and one shared destroyed flying with No 12 Group's Big Wing during the Battle of Britain. Following a staff tour, he joined No 167 Squadron on 9 December 1942 as its CO, but Lane was posted missing in action off the Dutch coast just four days after taking charge. He had claimed six and two shared destroyed, two unconfirmed destroyed and one probable by the time of his death.

Sqn Ldr 'Sandy' Lane in his Spitfire I P9386/QV-K, leads his wing into action against a 250-strong raid by the Luftwaffe on the London docks on 11 September 1940.

DOUGLAS BADER

Squadron Leader

Already a legendary figure within Fighter Command by the summer of 1940, Bader had returned to the cockpit in October 1939, eight years after he had lost both legs in a flying accident whilst at the controls of a Bulldog. Posted initially to No 19 Squadron and then on to No 222 Squadron (both flying Spitfire Is from Duxford) as a flight commander, Bader claimed his first victory on 1 June 1940 with the unit when he downed a Bf109 near Dunkirk. Promoted to acting squadron leader shortly thereafter, he was given command of Hurricane-equipped No 242 Squadron at Coltishall. Bader's unit subsequently saw considerable action flying as part of No 12 Group and he was credited with nine victories during the Battle of Britain. Having helped to champion Big Wing tactics during the late summer of 1940, Bader was posted to Tangmere as its first Wing Commander Flying in March 1941. Flying Spitfire IIs and Vs, he had claimed 10.5 victories and one probable by the time he was brought down in a mid-air collision over France on 9 August 1941. Bader spent the rest of the war as a PoW.

Sgt Bohumir Furst is greeted by the No 310 Squadron mascot shortly after returning to Duxford following a successful mission on 7 September.

Flt Sgt George 'Grumpy' Unwin and his Alsatian 'Flash'. The leading ace of No 19 Squadron in 1940, he too enjoyed success with the Big Wing on 7 September. Separated from his Flight, he thought attack was the best form of defence and hit five Bf 109s, claiming two of them destroyed.

No 19 Squadron's X4474 has its guns tended at RAF Fowlmere in late September 1940.

Enjoying a smoke and a chat on 21 September, pilots relax with their pets at Duxford's satellite airfield, RAF Fowlmere.

BACK THEM UP!

Hurricane Is of No 85 Squadron are seen in tight sections over Kent, led by Sqn Ldr Peter Townsend, September 1940.

The severed tail section of Do 17Z Wk-nr 2361 of 1./KG 76 lays on the roof of a house in Vauxhall Bridge Road on 15 September 1940. Probably the most famous aircraft to have crashed in Britain during World War 2, the centre section of the aeroplane came down near Victoria Station.

On 22 October 1940 HRH Princess Elizabeth (right) made her first radio broadcast at the age of just 14, with her sister Princess Margaret.

The Palace of Westminster appears in silhouette against a burning night sky during the Blitz.

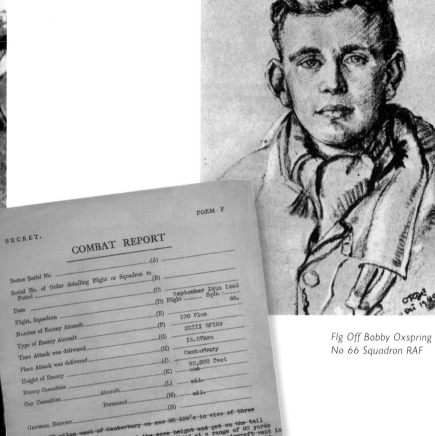

*Flg Off Bobby Oxspring
No 66 Squadron RAF*

FORM F

COMBAT REPORT

Sector Serial No. .... (A) ....

Serial No. of Order detailing Flight or Squadron to (B) ....
Patrol .... (C) ....

Date .... (D) September 18th 1940

Flight, Squadron .... (E) Flight : .... Sqdn. : 66.

Number of Enemy Aircraft .... (F) 100 Plus

Type of Enemy Aircraft .... (G) HEIII & ME109

Time Attack was delivered .... (H) 12.27hrs

Place Attack was delivered .... (J) Canterbury

Height of Enemy .... (K) 22,000 feet

Enemy Casualties .... (L) one nil.

Our Casualties ... Aircraft .... (M) nil.

... Personnel .... (N)

GENERAL REPORT ....

When 20 miles west of Canterbury we saw ME 109's in vics of three
flying at 22,000 feet. I was at the same height and got on the tail
of a 109 ,followed it through cloud and fired at a range of 80 yards
with a two second burst,and firing 240 rounds.The enemy aircraft went in
to a vertical dive with a long trail of white vapour,which I thought
was glycol fumed.After that I did not see the enemy aircraft again and
it was noted that the 109's had yellow noses,but no yellow wingtips.

Signature   R.W. Oxspring F/O.

O.C. .... Section
Flight
Squadron .... Squadron No. 66.

The recovery and scrapping of downed German aircraft in 1940 involved both civilian gangs and military personnel.

Tracer rounds arc their way towards an He 111 during a raid on London. This gun camera film is from the Spitfire of No 609 Squadron pilot Flt Lt J. H. G. McArthur.

A lone pilot from No 85 Squadron dons his parachute at RAF Debden on a fine October morning.

This famous retouched still from a roll of gun camera film captures the dramatic demise of an He 111.

Pilot Officer L.W. Stevens in his Hurricane I, N2359/YB-J, Debden, August 1940.

Wreckage of He 111H Wk-nr 2648 of 2./KG 55, which crash-landed on Selsey's East Beach on 11 July 1940 following an attack by No 145 Squadron Hurricanes.

Messerschmitt Bf 109E-7 'White 14' Wk-nr 3579 was flown by future Luftwaffe 'Experten' Hans-Joachim Marseille during the Battle of Britain. Marseille went on to score 158 victories before being killed in North Africa in 1942.

JOSEF FRANTIŠEK

Sergeant

The ranking RAF ace of the Battle of Britain, Czech Josef František had escaped to Poland after his country was invaded by Germany in 1938. Having flown with both the Czech and Polish air forces, he fled to Rumania when Poland fell. Escaping internment, he reached France via North Africa in October 1939. Electing to remain with the exiled Poles in the Armée de l'Air, František saw little or no combat before France fell and he headed to Britain. After completing his conversion training, he was assigned to No 303 'Polish' Squadron at Northolt and claimed his first victory on 2 September. An ill-disciplined pilot, he was seen as a danger to his colleagues when flying in formation. Eventually, his CO decided that it was best for František to be left to do his own thing, flying as a 'guest' of No 303 Squadron. Thus, František fought his own private war, accompanying the squadron into the air, but peeling off to fly a lone patrol over Kent in the area through which he knew German aircraft would be returning home. This tactic worked, for by the time František was killed in a flying accident on 8 October 1940, his score had reached 17 victories.

Three of No 303 'Polish' Squadron's leading pilots during the Battle of Britain at RAF Northolt, September 1940. Flg Off Zdzislaw Henneberg, Flt Lt Johnny Kent and Plt Off Marian Pisarek claimed 19 victories between them during a five-week period from 31 August to 5 October.

No 310 'Czech' Squadron pilots relax between missions at RAF Duxford, September 1940. The unit claimed 35 victories during the eight days it engaged the enemy in the Battle of Britain. Hurricane P3143, parked in the background, was written off in a training accident near Ely on 16 October 1940 that killed its pilot, Sgt Jan Chalupa.

No 19 Squadron made use of 21 X-serial range Spitfire Is between 1 July and 15 October 1940, featuring underwing roundels near the wingtips — a non-standard location.

"........ but for Heaven's sake don't say I told you!"

CARELESS TALK
COSTS LIVES

you never know who's listening!

CARELESS TALK
COSTS LIVES

15 September

On 15 September the Battle of Britain reached its climax as Göring authorised one final attempt to destroy Fighter Command – the Luftwaffe would subsequently never again be seen in such numbers over southern England. Although misty to start with, this cleared quickly and the sun shone through clear and bright. The first raid took place at 11.00hrs when fighter-bombers of II./KG 2 made a diversionary attack aimed at getting as many No 11 Group units into the air as possible with just 25 Do 17s, 21 Bf 109 Jabos (fighter-bombers) and more than 100 fighter escorts. An astonishing 254 Spitfires and Hurricanes were sent aloft to deal with this first incursion, with No 12 Group contributing its Big Wing to the action. For the first time since the start of the Battle of Britain, there were now greater numbers of defenders than there were attackers.

Having mauled this first attack, the RAF fighters returned to their bases to refuel and rearm just as Kesselring's main thrust for the day was forming up over Calais. This would consist of 114 He 111s, Do 17s and Ju 88s from nine Kampfgruppen, escorted by an astonishing 340 Bf 109s and 20 Bf 110s. Göring had recommended three fighters for every bomber at the start of Operation 'Loge', and Kesselring had gone one better. On this occasion, some of the Bf 109s were allowed to fly higher and faster than the bombers as they had done in the early stages of the campaign. Park, realising the size of this attack as it entered radar range, decided to send in smaller attacks before committing the bulk of his force just as the fighter escorts were forced to turn for home due to low fuel. The first British fighters – just 27 of them – made contact shortly after 14.00hrs...

One of the pilots scrambled on 15 September was Plt Off H. R. 'Dizzy' Allen of No 66 Squadron, based at Gravesend airport:

'The telephone screeched, the airman rotated his finger. There was always a sound and fury to a squadron scramble. There was a crackle of Merlins starting up the roar as the propellers began to rotate, dust blowing from behind the Spitfires, white smoke billowing from the exhaust stubs, airmen running, pilots jog-trotting, starter batteries being pulled out of harm's way, chocks being heaved away and pilots roaring their engines as they moved out of line. Briggs helped me to buckle on the parachute and Jones helped me to get the safety harness attached when I was in the cockpit. I set up the compass, checked that the pneumatic pressure was okay, oil pressure good and high, glycol temperature normal enough, waved the chocks away and moved out of line. I was senior enough now to have my own Spitfire, and Jones and Briggs were in my permanent possession. These occasions in 1940 were the last days of the knight and his squires so to speak. We were a good team, Jones, Briggs and myself, and I was about the fastest of them all to get my Spitfire moving for take-off.

'I closed on Jasper's (Sqn Ldr R. H. A. Leigh) starboard wing as he began to climb to the north.

'"Fibus leader: 100+ crossing in at Dover, Angels one-five upwards", the controller stated over the R/T.

'"Understood", Jasper replied. "We are at Angels one-five north of Gravesend, beginning a turn on to southerly heading."

'"Understood . Vector one-six-zero. Make Angels two-five."

'I hung high above Jasper's Spitfire as we made a lazy turn to port. Below lay London, the Thames sweeping in serpent-like fashion through its very heart. The cement works on the Thames issued clouds of white smoke, the docks looked awfully empty. Then I saw Canterbury coming towards us with its great Gothic cathedral where Thomas Beckett was murdered, which made me feel murderous towards the Teutonic gentlemen who were wrecking part of Britain's heritage with great regularity.

'"Fibus leader. Squadron smoking", came the voice of George [Plt Off G H Corbett].

'"Understood", Jasper replied. "Losing height".

'He wanted to keep us out of the contrail area and remain relatively invisible to German eyes – and God knows there were enough such eyes peering in our direction. We lost a bit of height and the controller vectored us towards the raid.

'"Lose height to Angels one-five", the controller requested.

'He wanted to try and put us among the bombers. We went into a slow dive and were now in battle formation.

'"Bandits ahead – above and below", came the voice of "Pickles" [Plt Off J. H. Pickering], who had the longest sight in the squadron.

'"Understood", Jasper replied. "Am continuing to low height".

'I saw nothing for about 30 seconds, then I saw black spots, which

quickly transformed themselves into many bombers, with fighters around them, and other fighters leaving tiny contrails high above. There must have been 300 in the balbo and there were 12 of us. What was more they couldn't yet have been intercepted by any other squadrons as they seemed to be in cohesive formations. We were below them by now, approaching them head-on. I turned the gun button to Fire.

'What Jasper thought he was doing I will never know, but it worked. He simply climbed the squadron into the middle of them. Incredibly, there were no mid-air collisions, nor was there much time for me to do more than give them a couple of squirts with the Brownings. A German bomber whizzed past my head a few feet away. I could see the bomb-aimer in the perspex nose of the Heinkel. A few yards away, a couple of Me 109s with dirty great yellow noses flashed past.

'Then there was nothing, nothing at all. It is unbelievable how at one moment the sky can be filled with aircraft and then they all vanish. But I knew where they were going, so I hauled back on the stick and broke the seal on the throttle quadrant to gain maximum emergency power. The Merlin shuddered under the boost and black smoke streamed from the exhausts. I caught up with a Heinkel which was struggling – small wonder, as Jasper's unconventional attack had split the balbo up to no mean extent. I gained height on it and then throttled back on the dive in case the Merlin blew up through excessive boost. The de Wilde incendiaries hit the port engine a lucky strike I guess, and the engine blew up, whereupon the aircraft began to cartwheel. I confirmed that it was a Heinkel 111, which meant that I had probably killed five men.

'I gave the Merlin emergency boost once again and found a Dornier 17. My bullets hit one of the engines and filthy black oil came back like a whiplash covering my windshield to the extent I could see nothing any longer through my gunsight. I half-rolled out of it, got down to treetop level and opened my canopy and nursed the Merlin back to Gravesend.

'The squadron claimed 12 German aircraft destroyed on that sortie, but how accurate those claims were I do not know.'

The formation encountered by No 66 Squadron consisted of fighters and bombers flying in three parallel columns three miles apart that stretched for 30 miles. As the bombers got closer to London – they were targeting Royal Victoria, West India and Surrey commercial docks in eastern London – Park scrambled every squadron at his disposal in No 11 Group, totalling 185 fighters from 19 squadrons.

Prime Minister Churchill had chosen to visit No 11 Group operations room at RAF Uxbridge that day, and he later recalled:

'A subdued hum arose from the floor where the busy plotters pushed their discs to and fro in accordance with the swiftly changing situation. Air Vice-Marshal Park gave general directions for the disposition of his fighter force, which were translated into detailed orders to each fighter squadron by a youngish officer in the centre of the Dress Circle. Park himself walked up and down behind, watching with vigilant eye every move in the game, supervising his junior executive's hand, and only occasionally intervening with some decisive order, usually to reinforce a threatened area.

'I became conscious of the anxiety of the commander, who now stood still behind his subordinate's chair. Hitherto, I had watched in silence. I now asked, "What other reserves have we?" "There are none", said Air Vice-Marshal Park".'

Shortly before 15.00hrs No 12 Group's Big Wing engaged the enemy aircraft just as the Bf 109 escorts started to turn back due to low fuel. 'The German bombers were taking quite a beating from us on that day', Plt Off Bobby Oxspring of No 66 Squadron remembered:

'Every squadron in No 11 Group had intercepted and, at that moment, I saw Douglas Bader's wing of five squadrons – three of Hurricanes and two of Spitfires – coming in from Duxford in No 12 Group. That was the day Göring had said to his fighter pilots that the RAF is down to its last 50 Spitfires. But today they had run up against 19 squadrons for a start when they were on their way in, and then, when they got over London, with the Messerschmitt 109s running out of fuel, in comes Douglas Bader with 60 more fighters, and got stuck in'.

To further compound the bombers' problems, cloud was now obscuring their primary targets over London. Under constant harassment by RAF fighters, they duly dropped their ordnance on the southeastern corner of the capital as they turned for home. They continued to be attacked mercilessly all the way back over the Kent coast. On what would subsequently become know as Battle of Britain Day, the Luftwaffe had flown more than 1,000 sorties and lost 56 aircraft – the RAF had claimed an astonishing 185 victories and 40 probables. Fighter Command had in turn lost 29 aircraft and 12 pilots killed. No fewer than 136 Luftwaffe aircrew had been either killed or captured. The Germans had failed in their attempt to inflict a telling blow on the RAF.

THE ROCK AND THE STORM

The response to the 'Saucepans for Spitfires' drive was huge, although exactly how many of the pots and pans donated were actually melted down and turned into aeroplanes is open to debate.

Bf 109E-1 Wk-nr 4851 lies on its back near Queen Anne's Gate in Windsor Great Park after overturning during a forced landing on 30 September 1940. Oberleutnant Karl Fischer of 7./JG 27 survived despite the crushed canopy.

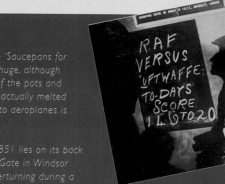

ROBERT FOSTER

Pilot Officer

South Londoner Bob Foster joined the RAF Volunteer Reserve in May 1939 and commenced his pilot training six months later after being called up. Sent to convert onto Hurricanes in early June 1940, he arrived at No 605 Squadron in No 13 Group a month later. Posted to Croydon with the unit on 7 September, he submitted a number of claims during the latter stages of the Battle of Britain. Following a spell as an instructor, he joined No 54 Squadron as a flight commander in April 1942 and was posted overseas with the unit two months later. Flying Spitfire VBs from austere strips in the northern Australian bush, Foster and his fellow pilots helped defend Darwin from Japanese attacks during the first half of 1943 – he was credited with four 'Betty' bombers and a 'Dinah' reconnaissance aircraft destroyed, two probables and two damaged during this period, earning him a DFC. Returning to Britain in February 1944, he saw out the rest of the war as a staff officer. Foster remained in the Royal Auxiliary Air Force until its disbandment in 1957.

Amongst the aces to fly Hurricane R4118 during 1940 was Plt Off Bob Foster, who used it to claim a Ju 88 damaged on 28 September and a share in the destruction of another Junkers bomber on 1 October.

After the debacle of 15 September Göring and his High Command could no longer claim that Fighter Command was on its knees. By nightfall the Germans had, in effect, lost the Battle of Britain. They did not know this, however, and neither did the British. Daylight bombing raids continued to be flown, though less frequently and in much smaller numbers. Heavier, more persistent and more destructive attacks on London and other British cities were now being made after dark, when the bombers did not have to worry about being intercepted by large numbers of Spitfires and Hurricanes.

Just 48 hours after Battle of Britain Day, Hitler postponed Operation 'Seelöwe' indefinitely. Nevertheless, Göring was allowed to continue his now favoured tactic of 'rolling' attacks, which he had introduced on 7 September, as and when the opportunity arose. Large-scale raids were mounted on 27 and 30 September, with London again being the principal target. Luftwaffe losses were high on both dates, with 57 aircraft being downed on the 27th and 43 on the 30th.

After the carnage of the previous three months, October 1940 provided the Luftwaffe and the RAF with some relief as the intensity of daylight missions dramatically tailed off. Indeed, there were only two major missions of note, involving mainly Ju 88s (the Do 17s and He 111s were now deemed to be too vulnerable for such operations in daylight), Bf 110s and swarms of Bf 109s – both fighters and fighter-bombers, the latter usually equipped with a single 500lb bomb. The Jabo aircraft were tasked with performing nuisance raids, each Jagdgeschwader having been ordered by Göring in late September to convert one third of its aircraft and pilots to the fighter-bomber role.

'Each wing provided the escort for its own bombers', Major Adolf Galland explained. 'The altitude for the approach was about 18,000ft. At the start we let the fighter-bombers fly in bomber formation, but it was soon apparent that the enemy fighters could concentrate fully on the Jabos. Therefore, we distributed the fighter-bombers in small units throughout the entire formation, and thus brought them in fairly safely over their target area. This type of raid had no more than nuisance value. The passive behaviour toward the enemy fighters, the feeling of inferiority when we were attacked, because of loss of speed, manoeuvrability, rate of climb, added to the unconvincing effort of single bombs scattered over wide areas, combined to ruin the morale of the German fighter pilot, already low because of the type of escorting that had to be done'.

Although the Jagdwaffe was at a low ebb, Fighter Command remained on high alert, particularly at the sharp end in No 11 Group as Sqn Ldr Sandy Johnstone of No 602 Squadron noted on 2 October:

'We are still on high alert. We are doing two, three, sometimes four sorties a day. People are coming back and falling asleep, sometimes on the floor at dispersal, or sitting upright in a chair. We are that tired. However, I may be wrong, but things seem to be easing off a bit these days. We only spot 109s cruising around at heights well above 30,000ft. These occasionally make furtive darts at us before soaring up again to their superior position, where they seem content to sit in a kind of haughty dignity. We gather the boys at Biggin Hill are finding the same thing. This sense of relaxation even seems to be permeating into the lives of the local civilians. Could it be that the Germans have had enough?'

Nevertheless, unsure whether small formations of nuisance raiders were the precursor to a large-scale attack, Fighter Command was kept on its toes throughout October. 'In fair weather they still came over two or three times a day', explained Sqn Ldr Harry Hogan of Kenley-based No 501 Squadron, who claimed three and one shared fighters destroyed and one probable during October. 'A formation of 50 109s could draw up practically the whole of our available force. You didn't know in advance whether they were fighters of bombers coming over. You were only given a patrol line or an interception course. Whether it was a bomber at the other end or a fighter carrying a bomb, you had no idea. Radar couldn't distinguish between them'.

Despite October being viewed as the quietest month of the Battle of Britain, Fighter Command had still lost 130 aircraft in combat and the Luftwaffe 340. Over the whole course of the campaign Fighter Command had had between 900 and 925 aircraft destroyed and just over 400 pilots killed. Between 1,590 and 1,740 German aeroplanes had been destroyed in combat. It had also suffered heavy personnel losses, losing five aircrew for every Fighter Command pilot killed.

Shortly after World War 2 had ended, 31 October 1940 was officially recognised as the end of the Battle of Britain, and unlike the previous 112 days, there were no combat losses experienced by either side. At the time, however, few people in Britain realised that the battle was over, as the devastating night Blitz would continue well into the spring of 1941. By then more than 30,000 civilians had been killed and scores more injured.

Although Prime Minister Winston Churchill delivered his famous speech in the House of Commons on 20 August 1940, the campaign was still very much in the balance. In the intervening years his immortal words have come to aptly sum up Fighter Command's role in defending Britain from invasion and ultimately changing the course of World War 2.

'The gratitude of every home in our Island,
in our Empire, and indeed throughout the world,
except in the abodes of the guilty,
goes out to the British airmen who, undaunted
by odds, unwearied in their constant challenge
and mortal danger, are turning the tide
of the World War by their prowess
and by their devotion...

Never in the field of human conflict was so much owed by so many to so few'

WINSTON CHURCHILL

Following Bomber Command raids on Italy, and keen to share in the glory of Britain's seemingly imminent defeat, Il Duce, Benito Mussolini, offered the Führer the use of aircraft from the Regia Aeronautica. The Corpo Aereo Italiano was duly formed on 10 September 1940, moving to bases in Belgium later that same month. It boasted eight squadrons of Fiat BR.20M bombers, a single squadron of Cant Z1007bis reconnaissance aircraft and six fighter units equipped with Fiat CR.42s and G.50s. Inexperienced, poorly equipped and unfamiliar with Luftwaffe tactical doctrine, the Italians only flew a handful of sorties. Daylight raids on Ramsgate were made on 29 October and 11 November, with the latter mission being intercepted by Hurricanes from No 46 Squadron and Stanford Tuck's No 257 Squadron. Five of the 10 BR.20Ms involved in the operation were shot down, as well as seven CR.42s. Tuck's men dubbed them 'The Chianti Raiders' and shared the spoils of war (above). The Corpo Aereo Italiano returned home in January 1941.

ACES *in* ART

'Suddenly a 109 comes past very fast with a Spitfire behind it. This is my chance. I get behind the Spitfire and centre it in my Revi. After a few shots it goes down. I watch it crash into the sea with a huge splash'

HELMUT WICK

HELMUT WICK

Major

Mannheim-born Helmut Wick joined the Luftwaffe in 1935 and was assigned to II./JG 134 after completing his flying training in 1937. Wick saw considerable combat from November 1939 through to 26 August 1940, claiming 22 victories. Awarded a Knight's Cross for his success, Wick briefly became Staffelkapitän of 6./JG 2 in early September, prior to being made Kommandeur of I./JG 2. On 6 October he became only the third fighter pilot to receive the Oakleaves to the Knight's Cross (his tally then stood at 41 victories) and two weeks later Wick became Kommandeur of JG 2 despite being only 25 years old. By now the most famous pilot in the Luftwaffe, he was shot down by No 609 Squadron ace Flt Lt John Dundas off the Isle of Wight on 28 November 1940 during his 168th combat mission. Although Wick was seen to bale out of his Bf 109E, JG 2's then ranking ace – he had taken his tally to 56 victories early in the mission – was never seen again.

Major Helmut Wick claims Plt Off Paul Baillon of No 609 Squadron as his 56th and last victim off The Needles, at the western end of the Isle of Wight, on the afternoon of 28 November 1940.

"If we are Mark'd to Die, we are enow
to do our Country Loss;
and if to Live, the Fewer the Men,
the Greater share of Honour"

King Henry the Fifth, Act IV, Scene III

William Shakespeare

Battle of Britain Losses
(10 July to 31 October 1940)

RAF Fighter Command

July – 68 aircrew and 91 aircraft
August – 176 aircrew and 389 aircraft
September – 173 aircrew and 358 aircraft
October – 120 aircrew and 185 aircraft

Luftwaffe

July – 348 aircrew and 185 aircraft
August – 993 aircrew and 694 aircraft
September – 829 aircrew and 629 aircraft
October – 492 aircrew and 379 aircraft

RAF Fighter Command Battle of Britain Pilot Nationalities

A total of 2,917 men were awarded the Battle of Britain clasp for having flown at least one authorised sortie with an eligible unit of Fighter Command between 10 July and 31 October 1940. They came from the following countries;

Great Britain 2,334
Australia 33
Belgium 29
Canada 98
Czechoslovakia 88
France 13
Ireland 10
Jamaica 1
New Zealand 126
Poland 145
Rhodesia 3
South Africa 25
United States of America 11

During the Battle of Britain 544 RAF aircrew lost their lives.

ROYAL AIR FORCE UNITS & TYPES

Spitfire I/II squadrons: Nos 19, 41, 54, 64, 65, 66, 72, 74, 92, 152, 222, 234, 266, 602, 603, 609, 610, 611, 616 and 421 Flt

Hurricane I squadrons: Nos 1, 1 (RCAF), 3, 17, 32, 43, 46, 56, 73, 79, 85, 87, 111, 145, 151, 213, 229, 232, 238, 242, 245, 249, 253, 257, 263, 302, 303, 310, 312, 501, 504, 601, 605, 607, 615, and 421 Flt, 422 Flt

Defiant I squadrons: Nos 141 and 264

Blenheim IF/IVF squadrons: Nos 23, 25, 29, 219, 235, 236, 248, 600, 604 and Fighter Interception Unit, Special Duties Flight

Gladiator I/II and Sea Gladiator squadrons: No 247, Shetland Fighter Flight, 804 NAS

BOULTON PAUL DEFIANT

Type: Single-engined monoplane fighter

Crew: Pilot and turret gunner

Dimensions:
Length: 35ft 4in (10.77m)
Wingspan: 39ft 4in (12m)
Height: 12ft 2in (3.7m)

Weights:
Empty: 6,078lb (2,757kg)
Max T/O: 8,318lb (3,773kg)

Performance:
Max Speed: 304mph (489km/h)
Range: 465 miles (748km)
Powerplant: Rolls-Royce Merlin III
Output: 1,030hp (768kW)
Armament: Four 0.303in machine guns in dorsal turret
First Flight: 11 August 1937
Production: 1,075

BRISTOL BLENHEIM IVF

Type: Twin-engined monoplane day/night fighter

Crew: Pilot, navigator and turret gunner

Dimensions:
Length: 39ft 9in (12.12m)
Wingspan: 56ft 4in (17.17m)
Height: 9ft 10in (3m)

Weights:
Empty: 8,840lb (4,010kg)
Max T/O: 12,500lb (5,670kg)

Performance:
Max Speed: 278mph (447km/h)
Range: 1,050 miles (1,690km)
Powerplants: 2 x Bristol Mercury VIII
Output: 840hp (626 kW) per engine
Armament: One 0.303-in machine guns in port engine nacelle, one in dorsal turret and four in underfuselage tray
First Flight: 12 April 1935 (Type 142)
Overall Production: 4,422

HAWKER HURRICANE I

Type: Single-engined monoplane fighter

Crew: Pilot

Dimensions:
Length: 31ft 5in (9.58m)
Wingspan: 40ft (12.19m)
Height: 13ft (3.96m)

Weights:
Empty: 4,982lb (2,260kg)
Max T/O: 7,490lb (3,397kg)

Performance:
Max Speed: 324mph (521km/h)
Range: 600 miles (965km)
Powerplant: Rolls-Royce Merlin II/III
Output: 1,030hp (768kW)
Armament: Eight 0.303in machine guns in wings
First Flight: 6 November 1935
Overall Production: 14,583

SUPERMARINE SPITFIRE IA

Type: Single-engined monoplane fighter

Crew: Pilot

Dimensions:
Length: 29ft 11in (9.12m)
Wingspan: 36ft 10in (11.23m)
Height: 11ft 5in (3.48m)

Weights:
Empty: 4,810lb (2,182kg)
Loaded Weight: 5,844lb (2,651kg)

Performance:
Max Speed: 355mph (571km/h)
Range: 575 miles (925km)
Powerplant: Rolls-Royce Merlin II/III
Output: 1,030hp (768kW)
Armament: Eight 0.303in machine guns
First Flight: 5 March 1936
Overall Production: 20,351

LUFTWAFFE UNITS & TYPES

Bf 109E units: Jagdgeschwaders 2, 3, 26, 27, 51, 52, 53, 54, 77 and LG 2   **Bf 110C/D units:** Erprobungsgruppe 210, LG 1, ZGs 2, 26, 76, Aufklärungsgruppe 14, 22, 31, 121 and 122

He 111P/H units: Kampfgeschwaders 1, 3, 4, 26, 27, 53, 55, Kampfgruppe 100, 126, Aufklärungsgruppe 120, 121, 122   **He 59C/D units:** Seenotstaffels 1 and 2

Ju 88A units: Kampfgeschwaders 1, 4, 30, 40, 51, 54, 76, 77, Lehrgeschwader 1, Kampfgruppe 806, Aufklärungsgruppe 120, 121, 122 and 123

Do 17P/Z units: Kampfgeschwaders 2, 3, 76, 77, Aufklärungsgruppe 10, 11, 14, 22, 31, 120, 121, 122, 123 and 124   **Ju 87B/R units:** Stukageschwaders 1, 2, 3, 76, 77, Trägergruppe 186 and Lehrgeschwader 1

DORNIER DO 17Z	HEINKEL HE 111P	JUNKERS JU 87B STUKA	JUNKERS JU 88A	MESSERSCHMITT BF 109E	MESSERSCHMITT BF 110C
Type: Twin-engined monoplane bomber	Type: Twin-engined monoplane bomber	Type: Single-engined monoplane dive-bomber	Type: Twin-engined monoplane bomber	Type: Single-engined monoplane fighter	Type: Twin-engined monoplane fighter/fighter-bomber
Crew: Pilot, navigator, bomb aimer/gunner and flight engineer/gunner	Crew: Pilot, navigator, bomb aimer, ventral and dorsal gunners	Crew: Pilot and rear gunner	Crew: Pilot, navigator, bomb aimer/gunner and flight engineer/gunner	Crew: Pilot	Crew: Two-/three-man crew
Dimensions:	Dimensions:	Dimensions:	Dimensions:	Dimensions:	Dimensions:
Length: 51ft 10in (15.8m)	Length: 53ft 9.5in (16.4m)	Length: 36ft 5in (11.10m)	Length: 47ft 2in (8.43m)	Length: 28ft (8.55m)	Length: 39ft 8.5in (12.10m)
Wingspan: 59ft 1in (18m)	Wingspan: 74ft 1.75in (22.6m)	Wingspan: 45ft 3.25in (13.80m)	Wingspan: 65ft 10.50in (20.08m)	Wingspan: 32ft 4.5in (9.87m)	Wingspan: 53ft 4.75in (16.27m)
Height: 15ft 0in (4.56m)	Height: 13ft 1.5in (4m)	Height: 13ft 2in (4.01m)	Height: 15ft 11in (4.85m)	Height: 8ft 2in (2.49m)	Height: 11ft 6in (3.50m)
Weights:	Weights:	Weights:	Weights:	Weights:	Weights:
Empty: 11,486lb (5,210kg)	Empty: 17,760lb (8,015kg)	Empty: 5,980lb (2,713kg)	Empty: 16,975lb (7,699kg)	Empty: 4,189lb (1,900kg)	Empty: 9,920lb (4,500kg)
Max T/O: 19,482lb (8,837kg)	Max T/O: 29,762lb (13,500kg)	Max T/O: 9,369lb (4,250kg)	Max T/O: 22,840lb (10,360kg)	Max T/O: 5,875lb (2,665kg)	Normal loaded: 15,300 lb (6,940kg)
Performance:	Performance:	Performance:	Performance:	Performance:	Performance:
Max Speed: 255mph (410km/h)	Max Speed: 200mph (322km/h)	Max Speed: 211mph (339km/h)	Max Speed: 292mph (470km/h)	Max Speed: 348mph (560km/h)	Max Speed: 349mph (561km/h)
Range: 628 miles (1,010km)	Range: 1,224 miles (1,970km)	Range: 490 miles (788km)	Range: 1,696 miles (2,730km)	Range: 410 miles (660km)	Range: 565 miles (909km)
Powerplant: Two BMW-Bramo 323P Fafnirs	Powerplant: Two Daimler-Benz DB601A-1s	Powerplant: Junkers Jumo 211Da	Powerplant: Two Junkers Jumo 211Bs	Powerplant: Daimler-Benz DB601Aa	Powerplants: Two Daimler-Benz DB601A-1 engines
Output: 1,972hp (1472kW)	Output: 2,200hp (1,640kW)	Output: 1,100hp (820kW)	Output: 2,400hp (1,790kW)	Output: 1,175hp (876kW)	Output: 2,200hp (1,640kW)
Armament: Up to eight MG15 7.92mm machine guns in nose, rear upper cockpit, cockpit sides and ventral gondola; maximum bomb load of 2,205lb (1,000kg) in bomb-bay	Armament: Six or seven MG15 7.92mm machine guns in nose, beam, dorsal, ventral and (optional) tail positions; maximum bomb load of 4,410lb (2,000kg) in bomb-bay	Armament: Two fixed MG17 7.92mm machine guns in wings and one MG15 7.92mm machine guns on flexible mounting in rear cockpit; maximum bomb load of 1,102lb (500kg) on centreline and four 110lb (50kg) bombs under wings	Armament: Five or six MG15 7.92mm machine guns in nose, rear cockpit and ventral gondola; maximum bomb load of 4,409lb (2,000kg) in bomb-bay and on underwing racks	Armament: Two 7.9mm machine guns in upper cowling, two 20mm cannon in wings; some E-3s additional 20mm cannon in propeller hub; fighter-bomber variant provision for carriage of one 551lb (250kg) bomb under fuselage	Armament: Two 20mm cannon and four 7.9mm machine guns in nose cowling, 7.9mm machine gun in rear cockpit; C-4/B fighter-bomber variant, maximum load of 1,102lb (500kg) bombs carried externally; C-7, maximum load of 2,205lb (1,000kg) bombs
First Flight: Autumn 1934	First Flight: 24 February 1935	First Flight: Late 1935	First Flight: 21 December 1936	First Flight: 29 May 1935	First Flight: 12 May 1936
Production: 2,139	Production: 6,508	Production: 6,500	Production: More than 7,000 Ju 88As (all variants) were built	Production: Approximately 4,000 E-models	Production: 6,170

Acknowledgements

A work such as this is only made possible through the passion, assistance and imagination of many individuals. John Dibbs would like to thank, Tom Neil, Allan Burney, Winston Ramsey, Phil Hempell, Iain Dougall, Alessandro Taffetani, Uwe Glaser, Tony Parsons, Robin Brooks, Peter Arnold, Jim, Bob and Scott Donovan at Kenmore Camera, Harald Rabeder, Kent Ramsey, Mike Gurley at Canon. Also Tony Holmes for his amazing knowledge and text. Pam Dibbs has inspired and encouraged me to make these dreams fly. Thank you.

Many thanks also to the aircraft owners, operators, pilots and restorers that make the sight and sound of a Spitfire or Hurricane a reality in our skies today and for generations to come – Sqn Ldr Al Pinner and Sqn Ldr Dunc Mason at The Battle of Britain Memorial Flight, John Romain and all at Historic Flying, Peter Monk and all at Biggin Hill Heritage Hangar, Jan Friso Roosen, The Friedkin Family, Ed and Fran Russell, Peter and Polly Vacher, Thomas Kaplan and the late Simon Marsh.

Pilots who flew for the project – John Romain, Paul Bonhomme, Alan Walker, Lee Proudfoot, Richard Grace, Carl Schofield, Flt Lt Anthony Parkinson, Sqn Ldr Dunc Mason. Camerashop pilots were Tim Ellison, Peter Monk, Richard Verrall, Andy Hill and David Frasca.

Special thanks to Simon Smith and Alex Hamilton for creating the amazing art that brings the battle to life.
Prints are available of the art featured in this book from –
Simon Smith - www.sasmithart.co.uk
Alex Hamilton - www.alexhamilton.net

I must express my gratitude to Adrian Cox, Ann Saundry and Nigel Price at Key Publishing for joining in the vision to create this book. Iain Dougall for his enthusiasm, support and invaluable assistance on the project. Allan Burney worked many unsociable hours to help me create this work and to him I am indebted for his friendship and resilient spirit.

Lastly, let us all thank the Few and the Many that endured the difficult and dark times of 1940 and beyond. We now know it was their Finest Hour.

Bibliography

Allen, Wg Cdr H R 'Dizzy', *Battle for Britain* (Corgi, 1975); Bickers, Richard T, *Ginger Lacey – Fighter Pilot* (Pan Books, 1969); Boiten, Theo, *Bristol Blenheim* (Crowood, 1998); Bowyer, Chaz, *Bristol Blenheim* (Ian Allan, 1984); Bowyer, Michael J F, *Aircraft for the Few* (PSL, 1991); Bungay, Stephen, *The Most Dangerous Enemy* (Aurum, 2000); Caldwell, Donald, *The JG 26 War Diary, Vol 1* (Grub Street, 1996); Caldwell, Donald, *JG 26 Photographic History* (Airlife, 1994); Cull, Brian, Bruce Lander with Heinrich Weiss, *Twelve Days in May* (Grub Street, 1995); Cornwall, Peter D, *The Battle of France Then and Now* (After Battle, 2007); Deighton, Len, *Battle of Britain* (Jonathan Cape Ltd, 1980); Dibbs, John and Tony Holmes, *Hurricane – A Fighter Legend* (Osprey, 1995); Drake, Billy with Christopher Shores, Billy Drake, *Fighter Leader* (Grub Street, 2002); Foreman, John, *Battle of Britain – The Forgotten Months* (Air Research Publications, 1988); Foreman, John, *RAF Fighter Command Victory Claims of World War Two Part One 1939-1940* (Red Kite, 2003); Foreman, John, *1941 – The Turning Point - Part 1 the Battle of Britain to the Blitz* (Air Research Publications, 1993); Forrester, Larry, *Fly For Your Life* (Panther Books, 1968); Franks, Norman, *RAF Fighter Command Losses of the Second World War* (Midland Publishing Ltd, 1997); Franks, Norman, *Air Battle Dunkirk* (Grub Street, 2000); Galland, Adolf, *The First and the Last* (Fontana, 1971); Gelb, Norman, *Scramble* (Michael Joseph, 1986); Goss, Chris, *The Luftwaffe Bombers' Battle of Britain* (Crécy, 2000); Goss, Chris, *The Luftwaffe Fighters' Battle of Britain* (Crécy, 2000); Green, William, *Warplanes of the Third Reich* (Doubleday, 1972); Halley, James, *The K File – The Royal Air Force of the 1930s* (Air-Britain, 1995); Holmes, Tony, Osprey Aircraft of the Aces 18 – *Hurricane Aces 1939-40* (Osprey, 1998); Holmes, Tony, Osprey Duel 5 – *Spitfire I/II vs Bf 109E* (Osprey, 2007); Holmes, Tony, Osprey Duel 29 – *Hurricane I vs Bf 110* (Osprey, 2010); Holmes, Tony, *Images of War – American Eagles* (Pen & Sword, 2015); Jefford, C G, *RAF Squadrons* (Airlife, 2001); Lake, Jon, *The Battle of Britain* (Silverdale Books, 2000); Mason, Francis K, *Battle Over Britain*, (Aston Publications, 1990); Mathews, Andrew and John Foreman, *Luftwaffe Aces – Biographies and Victory Claims, Vols 1-4* (Red Kite, 2014) ; Moore, Kate, *The Battle of Britain* (Osprey, 2010); Morgan, Eric B and Edward Shacklady, *Spitfire – The History* (Key Publishing, 1987); Obermaier, Ernst, *Die Ritterkreuzträger der Luftwaffe Jagdflieger 1939-1945* (Verlag Dieter Hoffmann, 1966); Parker, Nigel, *Luftwaffe Crash Archive, Vols 1-6* (Red Kite, 2013-15) ; Price, Dr Alfred, *World War II Fighter Conflict* (Purnell, 1975); Price, Dr Alfred, *The Hardest Day* (BCA, 1979); Ramsey, Winston (editor), *The Battle of Britain Then and Now Mk IV* (After The Battle, 1987); Ramsey, Winston (editor), *The Blitz Then and Now, Vols 1-2* (After The Battle, 1987-88); Saunders, Andy, *Stuka Attack!* (Grub Street, 2013); Saunders, Andy, *Spitfire Mark I P9374* (Grub Street, 2012); Shores, Christopher and Clive Williams, *Aces High* (Grub Street, 1994); Stedman, Robert F, Osprey Men-at-Arms 377 – *Luftwaffe Air & Ground Crew 1939–45* (Osprey, 2002); Stedman, Robert F, Osprey Warrior 122 – *Jagdflieger: Luftwaffe Fighter Pilot 1939-45* (Osprey 2008); Thomas, Andrew, Osprey Aircraft of the Aces 105 – *Defiant, Blenheim and Havoc Aces* (Osprey, 2012); Thomas, Nick, *Hurricane Squadron Ace* (Pen & Sword, 2014); Townsend, Peter, *Duel of Eagles* (Weidenfeld, 1990); Vacher, Peter, *Hurricane R4118* (Grub Street, 2005); Vasco, John J and Peter D Cornwall, *Zerstörer – The Messerschmitt 11 and its Units in 1940* (JAC Publications, 1995); Vasco, John J, *Luftwaffe Colours Zerstörer Volume One – Luftwaffe Fighter-Bombers and Destroyers 1936-1940* (Classic Publications, 2005); Weal, John, Osprey Combat Aircraft 1 – *Junkers Ju 87 Stukageschwader 1937-41* (Osprey, 1997); Weal, John, Osprey Combat Aircraft 17 – *Ju 88 Kampfgeschwader on the Western Front* (Osprey, 2000); Weal, John, Osprey Combat Aircraft 91 – *He 111 Kampfgeschwader in the West* (Osprey, 2012); Weal, John, Osprey Aircraft of the Aces 25 – *Messerschmitt Bf 110 Zerstörer Aces of World War 2* (Osprey, 1999); Weal, John, Osprey Aviation Elite Units 1 – *Jagdgeschwader 2 'Richthofen'* (Osprey, 2000); Weal, John, Osprey Aviation Elite Units 22 – *Jagdgeschwader 51 'Mölders'* (Osprey, 2006); Weal, John, Osprey Aviation Elite Units 25 – *Jagdgeschwader 53 'Pik-As'* (Osprey, 2007); Wynn, Kenneth G, *Men of the Battle of Britain* (CCB, 1999); Website; Aces of the Luftwaffe – www.luftwaffe.cz; Guglielmetti, di Luca and Andea Rebora, *La Regia Aeronautica nella Battaglia d'Inghilterra* (Ufficio Storico Aeronautica Militare, 2014)